HOW TO EMPOWER PEOPLE AT WORK

'It is not enough to learn management techniques – they [managers] must also have the right conditions to grow and flourish.'

Radha (1991), *The Zen Way to be an Effective Manager,*
Management Books 2000

Other works by the same author:

Practical Counselling Skills, Winslow Press
50 Activities for Managing Stress, Gower
50 Activities for Developing Counselling Skills in Managers, Gower
NLP Counselling: 'Magic in Action', Winslow Press
How to Identify and Manage Stress, MCB University Press
Coping with Stress in Caring, Blackwell Scientific
Stress and Coping in Nursing, Chapman Hall
Systematic Relaxation, Winslow Press

HOW TO EMPOWER PEOPLE AT WORK

A Guide to Becoming a Green-Fingered Manager

Roy Bailey, PhD, CPsychol, AFBPsS

Chartered Psychologist

lll.
2000

First published in 1995 by Management Books 2000 Ltd
125A The Broadway, Didcot, Oxfordshire OX11 8AW

Illustrations by Peter Harris

Printed and bound in Great Britain by WBC Book Manufacturers, Bridgend

British Library Cataloguing in Publication Data is available

ISBN 1-85252-235-6

Contents

Foreword

Mike, a sales and marketing director for a multi-national hi-tec company, had been charged with the task of implementing a major change programme within the UK operation. The initial phase of the exercise had been painful because it had involved a significant number of redundancies but that was now complete and he looked forward to the new tomorrow with enthusiasm and energy.

His enthusiasm was not echoed throughout the organisation. He complained that staff were coming to work late, leaving early, not completing tasks on time, taking more days off due to illness and complaining about all the new plans for the future. Mike was totally frustrated by the lack of enthusiasm, low morale, suspicion and general apathy that surrounded the organisation. He could not understand why this should be; he believed that these employees should be jumping for joy because they had a job.

Unfortunately Mike's view is held by senior management of many large organisations and is often light years away from the truth. Employees are not jumping for joy because they have a job. Many are suffering from what is now being recognised as 'Survivor Syndrome'. They may have a job, but for how long? They may feel guilty that they have survived the cutbacks but face increased work loads, added responsibilities, limited resources and certainly no acknowledgement for their increased efforts.

There is a feeling that organisations are experiencing a slow lingering death and have totally ignored that employees undergoing change need help and support. Many companies engaged in downsizing activities have paid conscience money to outplacement providers to maintain a good PR image but have scant resources to help the individuals who have to take the organisation forward to achieve high levels of success.

The black scenario painted by Mike is very common and gradually enlightened companies are being forced to recognise that this impasse has got to be addressed. The big question is how? Many organisations are searching for a solution and some are turning to the world of counselling to see if these techniques hold any clues.

Attitudes towards counselling are changing, especially as people experience problem-solving models of counselling which provide a pragmatic approach to individuals taking more responsibilities for their own growth and development. No longer is counselling seen as something only for wimps or those with problems. The value of counselling is being acknowledged as a positive intervention which facilitates the development of empathy, intuition, creative thinking, and successful change management. This helps to balance the more rigid, logical, analytical styles which have held such prominence in the past.

Practical Performance Counselling as defined by Roy Bailey is an excellent example of how counselling can provide an exciting and workable solution to many of the urgent issues facing organisations today. Organisations need employees to realise more and more of their potential; this can be successfully achieved by adopting a counselling approach.

I only wish Roy's book had been published when Mike was facing his problems. It would have provided an excellent vehicle to take his new business forward. From now on *How to Empower People at Work* will certainly be on my recommended book list.

Bridget A Wright,
Director, Professional Services, for Methven Career Developments Ltd.

Past Chair Association for Counselling at Work (ACW)
Member of the Management Committee, British Association for
Counselling (BAC)
Member of the Lead Body for Advice, Guidance, Counselling and
Psychotherapy

1

PRACTICAL PERFORMANCE COUNSELLING

'At last someone understands how it feels and seems to be me, without wanting to analyse or judge me. Now I can blossom, grow and learn.' *Carl Rogers*

The manager with 'green fingers'

Great managers have green fingers. They know how to grow people. They have the practical counselling skills to bring out the best in others. How many times have you heard that managers get things done through others? You could probably give many examples where you have been urged to develop or use your management skills.

The management skills of the green-fingered manager complement but go much farther and beyond the setting of objectives, conducting performance reviews and employee appraisals. They have developed practical counselling skills to empower people at work. To become a green-fingered manager you need to move on from being only task-oriented and become task-oriented plus. The 'plus' is the important but neglected part of managing. The plus is the difference between a mediocre manager and a manager who grows people.

Managers who grow people are what I call green-fingered managers. They don't wield the big stick and kick ass. Quite the reverse: they create conditions at work where employees blossom and discover untapped resources that achieve two main goals. The first is employees who are prized as people; the second is significantly increased morale, job satisfaction and performance at work. A green-fingered manager is a master gardener. Like a master gardener the green-fingered manager knows the soil and the plants that will grow in it. Most of all, great managers know how to create the conditions where people can learn to develop and grow and make the most of themselves and their abilities. Improved performance at work comes from releasing the latent potential of people. It means doing things *with* people, not *to* them. The first thing you need to do to become a green-fingered manager is to create the conditions where others *know* they can learn, grow and shine at work.

Growing and groaning during periods of change

Employees in many organizations perform at only 10-25 per cent of their capacity. Others may be working flat out but not achieving much for their efforts except a very high level of stress and job burnout. When an increase in performance is needed, as Charles Handy has observed, a redoubling of effort is often the result. Unfortunately, the efforts are often wrongly placed and fail to achieve agreed objectives. Why? Well, sometimes it will simply be that you have chosen irrelevant or unreachable and unrealistic objectives. But more often it is likely that the person needs to learn how to discover the new skills and personal competencies that are necessary for successful performance.

Alvin Toffler in his prophetic book *Future Shock* stated that we live and work in an age of rapidly accelerating change where the only constant is change itself. 'Standard solutions to standard problems' are no longer the norm. C. P. Snow, the novelist and futurist, has observed that until this century change did occur but it was so slow it went by largely unnoticed in our lifetime. Now the rate of change has accelerated so much that we can hardly keep up with it. The world of work is changing so fast that employees are suffering from low job satisfaction, poor morale, stress, absenteeism and poor job performance. There will be no letting up on the pressure to perform at work. The opposite seems to be the case. If anything we are driving to the future and our feet are 'flat to the boards'. Warren Bennis, the well-known social psychologist and author of the best-seller *Leaders,* says that 'No exaggeration, no hyperbole, no outrage can realistically describe the extent and pace of change.' In fact, only exaggerations appear to be true. If we fail to provide new opportunities for fresh learning and constructive actions within this vortex of change there will be serious consequences. For one, a person's motivation to work will be seriously threatened.

Mobilizing motivation

As long ago as the apparently safe and stable climate of 1968 Frederick Herzberg showed from an extensive study of engineers and accountants that simply providing security, status, comfortable conditions at work, supervision and attractive pay and salary packages was not a programme for increasing job satisfaction. At best, these were only what Herzberg called hygiene factors that resulted in low or lack of job dissatisfaction. In other words, employees might say they were not dissatisfied with their work but still experience low job satisfaction. The main reason for this conundrum is that what motivates people towards high job satisfaction is not hygiene factors but a sense of personal growth, personal worth, recognition, responsibility and recognized advancement at work. In other words, personal motivation is crucial to whether someone experiences job satisfaction at work. Cut out their motivators and we run the risk of running an uninterested, unenthusiastic and depressed workforce.

Hygiene factors and motivators at work

The index below combines hygiene factors and motivators for people at work. Check them out and write an 'H' against the statements you think are hygiene factors and an 'M' against those you consider to be motivators. When you have done this ask yourself how accurate you were. How does the pattern of your motivation relate to your work? You can also conduct this exercise with people at work and consider how their pattern of motivation affects their degree of job satisfaction/dissatisfaction.

Hygiene or Motivator?

1 A sense of personal achievement ....[ ]
2 Freedom to organize and manage own time ....[ ]
3 Job security ....[ ]
4 Company policy and administration ....[ ]
5 High salary ....[ ]
6 Recognition for work done well ....[ ]
7 Good relationships with peers at work ....[ ]
8 Opportunities for advancement/promotion ....[ ]
9 Personal development and growth ....[ ]
10 Supervision ....[ ]
11 A job with an important purpose ....[ ]
12 Participation in decision-making ....[ ]
13 Safe working conditions ....[ ]
14 Personal responsibility ....[ ]
15 Personal life ....[ ]

A sensitive combination of hygiene and motivator factors can help to create positive job attitudes among employees. However, it is important to appreciate that not every hygiene factor or motivator affects everyone in the same way. It is the green-fingered manager who has the responsibility and the challenge of helping people to find out how they can best be motivated and experience job satisfaction at work. The challenge for the manager is to help create the attitudes towards work which are reflected in average or outstanding job satisfaction and committed performance at work. Without a doubt it is managers who occupy this key position. They create the conditions under which people grow or stagnate at work.

Managers have at last started to discover that the way to ensure the success of their organization is not to dig in and try to retain outmoded methods of management and remain the same in a changing world. Those that have done this soon find that the world has passed them by – sometimes so much so that their industry has largely disappeared, is being gradually consumed or has been swallowed up by another organization.

There is an alternative. It is obvious: you can grow your own people in a way that satisfies them and at the same time increases the health, wealth and success of your organization. It may take time. It may be challenging and it may be painful at times. But where managers can create the conditions where employees can learn to become collaborative partners in the future of their organizations, they will have created a significant shift in the meaning of work.

Work itself should be the arena for the personal satisfaction and vibrant performance of people. If you accept anything less you will get less. Simply expecting employees to be happy, contented and outstanding at work – whatever they do – is wishful thinking. Being clear about what people have to achieve at work is important. Without it we demonstrate the wise Chinese proverb that if we don't know where we are going whatever road we travel on will do.

People and organizations need to know the direction they are travelling in. But equally if we are a band of unwilling travellers we will be a drag on the direction of the organization. Managers need to take audit and ask themselves if they are, as R. D Laing has said, 'ignoring the obvious' – and the obvious is that people are the source of all success. By creating the conditions for significant personal learning amongst employees in your organization, you increase the likelihood of its success.

How ready are you to take up this challenge? It requires your commitment and the practical counselling skills that facilitate and empower employees to deal with their problems at work and to make the most of themselves in their organization.

Planting people for growth and development

Motivation and commitment are not enough. Managers now know that simplistic recipes produce simplistic and disappointing results. Organizations need keen and enthusiastic employees. But energy must be redirected to get the desired results. Imagine that you need to find your car at night. It is parked in a car park; there are no lights. It is lost! What do you do? Do you fumble around in the dark trying to find your car or do you obtain a flashlight and direct the beam over each number plate until you find it? What else could you do?

This example is not about finding a right or wrong answer. What it does do, I hope, is to make you ask yourself the question, 'How do I use my energy?' The answer should be that you use it where you think you will get the best results in the circumstances. The circumstances are pretty obvious in the car park, but at work they may be more complex. This makes it all the more crucial for managers to examine the work that has to be done and the person best suited to carrying it out. Facilitating this is one of the essential contributions managers can make to people in organizations.

Planting people needs care and attention. Give them a job that is repetitive and too small for them and they become bored, uninterested and probably make costly errors. Over a long period of time people can become resentful and depressed. Others turn to outward expression of hostility and may even damage equipment and sabotage production. Mounting evidence from studies of stress at work supports this view. Many of these problems come from treating people simply as a machine that has to complete a specific task in a given period. The assembly line worker is at the mercy of the production line. Charlie Chaplin conveyed with tragic humour the plight of the assembly line worker in the classic silent movie 'Modern Times' – rushing when the pace was increased and idling when the pace was monotonous. Men and women are not machines. We create resentment and massive and often insurmountable personal problems when we treat them as if they were.

Studs Terkel in his book *Working* clearly points out some of the reactions people have when they are trapped in jobs that are too small for them or viewed simply as machines. "'I'm caged," says the bank-teller', "'I'm a machine," says the spot-welder', "'A monkey can do what I can do," says a receptionist'.

Up or down the organization, if people are planted in jobs that are too small for them they will feel undervalued, lack self-esteem, and have little confidence in themselves. Some find ways of inventing and dramatizing their situation and escaping from the meaninglessness of their work, like the lawyer who did conveyancing work all day long but spent a lot of time daydreaming and ended up producing a new electronic office system that took away the monotony of much of the work. But many people can't escape from their tedious prisons. It is here that managers can help facilitate new ways of doing old things, as well as new ways of doing new things – ways that free the individual to find dignity and power at work, whatever they do.

Charles Garfield, the clinical psychologist who has contributed greatly to our understanding of peak performance in sport and at work, notes that for any person self-management comes through self-mastery. But first: 'An individual must find meaning and a way to grow, or die on the job. So when I think of peak performers, I think of any person, in an organization or out, who discovers ways to be a distinct contributing person – who refuses to give in to the system merely because it initially looks impervious to any attempts to affect it.'

Using practical performance counselling skills managers can help individuals to find fresh energy, commitment and satisfactory solutions within work systems. The first thing you need to do is to learn to thrive on the rollercoaster.

On the rollercoaster and out of control

Much managerial work is conducted at a breakneck pace, a pace that may even have a clear direction but is carried out at a furious rate – a rate that may have an unpredictable pattern and comes in fits and starts. Planting people in these occupational conditions makes demands on them that they have little control over and are ill prepared to deal with. Marianne Frankenhauser reported the effects of systems and technology at work that render people with a sense of loss of control as a result of increasing the pace of work. In these conditions at work, people suffer from a stress spiral and alarm reactions which progressively interfere with their ability to plan, think and act in a coordinated and coherent way. You end up on a rollercoaster that is out of control.

As the rollercoaster speeds up so do your body and mind in an effort to keep up. Typical body reactions are a marked increase in blood pressure, sugar levels, stress hormones and heartbeat. The psychological effects can be seen in anger, anxiety, depression, poor sleep patterns, faulty memory and crippling concentration problems. The Rollercoaster Effect shows up in under-performance at work and in our personal lives. Poor decision-making, erratic actions and fragmented emotions are signs that we are on the rollercoaster and we don't know how to get off.

If we know how to stop the rollercoaster effect we won't want to get off. Managers need to know how to release the skills, competencies and motivation of people to ride the rollercoaster. They need to know how to empower people to challenge dull and uninteresting work. On the other hand, they need to know how to use the momentum and thrust of change to achieve personal satisfaction and organizational goals. To do this, you need to be prepared to enter a collaborative adventure with other employees so they can discover and unearth untapped skills and vital personal resources that will create quantum leaps in performance at work.

The first thing managers need to know is how to facilitate the personal learning of employees – the kind of learning that will be significant to each individual but at the same time create and contribute significantly more to their organization than at present. How can managers begin to make this happen? What road is likely to lead to this progress and satisfaction of individuals at work? The answer lies in managers acquiring and using practical performance counselling skills.

The road to performance counselling

In his seminal book *Freedom to Learn,* Carl Rogers identified the essential elements upon which powerful performance counselling can be built. He found that personal counselling has a significant impact on how we change, what we do, and what we learn. How far along the road to performance counselling are you as a manager? When you are working with a person on their performance, do you:

- Communicate warmth and positive regard?
- Communicate an openness to their views, thoughts, feelings and behaviour?
- Listen carefully and accurately?
- Provide them with rewarding feedback?
- Share bad news in a way where constructive action can be taken?
- Communicate in ways that reflect your own thoughts, feelings and behaviour?
- Think, say, feel and do what you mean?
- Become person-centred rather than self-centred?
- Maintain a sense of genuineness in your personal interactions with others?

Prizing people

When you create and communicate these conditions you stop being self-centred. You start prizing people and not simply their performance. Prizing people occurs by conveying to them that they are worthy; prizing people communicates the message 'I respect your contribution'; above all prizing people enables them to feel proud of their performance and to give their commitment, energies and abilities willingly to their job.

A word of warning. Prizing people is not a soft option. It sometimes means confronting them on aspects of their behaviour, treasured beliefs, rigid thinking and hidden feelings. However, this needs to be done in a way that gets the best out of the situation and conveys positive regard for their views and their feelings. Prizing people is not directionless 'touchy-feely' stuff; neither is it steam-rollering others into doing what you want them to do. Prizing people is seeing their future potential contribution and valuing their present performance.

When you prize people you provide opportunities for individuals to discover the freedom to learn. When you present people with the freedom to learn they will release themselves from their shackles and inhibitions, their fears and defences. When they can do that, 'miracles happen'. They will surprise you. What would you give to come into your office each day and be absolutely amazed at the things people were learning and how they were applying what they learned to their work? Wouldn't it be exciting? You can release the personal learning of people by adopting and practising performance counselling values, and the greatest prize is prizing people.

How to survive in the snake pit

There is a scene in the film 'Raiders of the Lost Ark' where Indiana Jones gets caught in a snake pit. Through great presence of mind and heroic composure he survives and lives to pursue his next adventure. Empowering people through performance counselling is like that. It is exciting, but it can also be like walking through a snake pit. You've got to watch where you put your feet. There are certain things you should do and others you must avoid. First those you should avoid.

- Avoid treating performance counselling as an opportunity to boss or order people around.
- Avoid approaching performance counselling as an opportunity to manipulate individuals or groups simply to meet your own needs.

- Avoid pretending to engage in performance counselling when you have a secret agenda or devious intentions.
- Avoid using performance counselling as a means to off-load and avoid your own responsibilities and goals.
- Avoid treating performance counselling as an excuse for inaction.
- Avoid practising performance counselling as if it were a soft option and does not involve careful thought, feelings and actions.

When you can avoid these dangers you will have gone a long way toward combating some of the most common mistakes in performance counselling. But you can go further than this: you can strengthen your approach to performance counselling by making sure that you:

- Convey respect, genuineness and positive regard during performance counselling.
- Attempt to understand personal and work issues as other people see them.
- Collaborate with others to make sense of their concerns, find appropriate solutions and take agreed action.
- Appreciate the values and motives that are linked to others' occupational and personal priorities.
- Understand that performance counselling is a process that takes time and is aimed at reaching future goals.
- Focus on the here and now of where people are and use this as a bridge to explore routes and paths to the future.
- Mobilize the present and as yet untapped personal resources of individuals and groups so they can be aligned to achieve their future goals.
- Expect the benefits of performance counselling to take effect – but remember, Rome wasn't built in a day. People take that little bit longer to build new habits and refreshing repertoires that lead to improved performance at work.

Practising what you preach and preaching what you practise

If you are to provide the conditions for prizing people so that they grow and excel in their performance you have to practise what you preach. You have to set an example of what it means to have the freedom to learn – even the freedom to make mistakes.

When you actually practise prizing people, when you motivate them as well as planting them in situations where they can grow, then you are well on the road to a powerful performance-building relationship with them. It will take time. But the rewards are high, and when you get them don't forget to tell people how well they are doing and let other managers know as well. Let them know that you prize people and it is they – not just their roles – who are important to you.

The importance of managers' prizing people has been stressed by Charles Handy in his book *The Age of Unreason*. He urges us to note that 'The new manager must be a different manager. He, and increasingly she, must use what in psychological jargon is called reinforcement theory, applauding success and forgiving failure; he or she must use mistakes as an opportunity for learning, something only possible if the mistake is truly forgiven because otherwise the lesson is heard as a reprimand and not an offer of help. The new manager must learn to specify the measures of success as well as the signs of failure and must then allow his or her people the space to get on with it in their own way. The new manager has to be teacher, counsellor and friend, as much as, or more than he or she is commander, inspector and judge. It is a major change in our ways of managing.'

When you prize people, practise what you preach and preach what you practise. You will have well equipped yourself with the principles of performance counselling. Your efforts to achieve them will have been worthwhile. So what is involved? When you are growing people and motivating people for top performance this practical performance counselling model is one that you should find helpful:

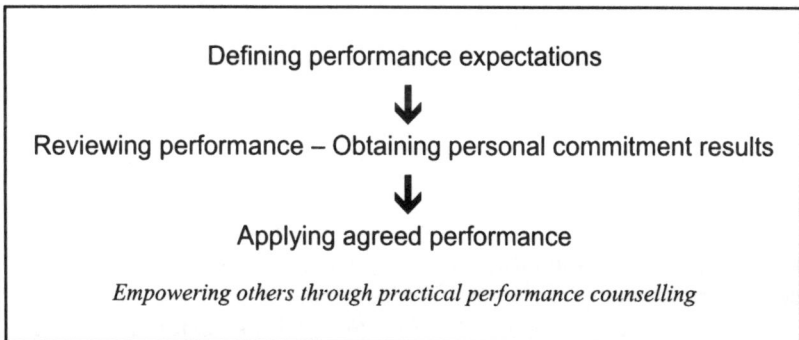

Defining performance expectations

↓

Reviewing performance – Obtaining personal commitment results

↓

Applying agreed performance

Empowering others through practical performance counselling

Defining performance expectations

Far too often managers and employee relations start here and get it wrong. It's not that they are wrong to try to achieve a *clear definition* of the performance expected. Without it, how can a manager or an employee know how well they are doing? The problem is how we go about defining the expectations and who defines the performance that is required.

Clearly, what is expected should be made explicit, specific and measurable if possible. By doing this you further reduce the risk of getting things badly wrong. Cutting down on error now will reduce the problems you have to face in the future. You can manage this by making it clear from the start what is expected from the person and their performance. By making sure you get it right from the start, you avoid having to make unnecessary changes of direction in the future.

Obtaining personal commitment

Unless you agree with others and share your expectations of each other, a number of problems can arise. First, you won't know where you are going. Second, you might think you agree when in fact there are different views of what should be done and how to do it. In this situation you will create a confusing communication cocktail for mis-understanding each other. A further difficulty is that you may fail to obtain the personal commitment of the individual employee or team.

Charles Margerison in his work with managers from many countries has observed that: 'Unless the manager and employee share and agree on expectations and reduce uncertainty to an acceptable level, they cannot achieve commitment. Yet the number of instances managers and employees fail to thoroughly discuss and agree on expectations is staggering.'

To achieve personal commitment is not something *you* do as a manager. This may sound surprising – but personal commitment has to come from the individual. It is the individual's decision to 'own' the performance expected from them that provides you with the knowledge they will do their utmost to achieve the goals they set with you. Simply imposing the performances expected from employees at best only gets compliance, and compliance is a poor second to personal commitment.

Peter Drucker recalled in *The Practice of Management* how we get in a bad way when we decide and set the performances that are required by an organization without involving the individual in the process. Personal commitment comes from the individual participating with you in deciding and setting the performance required to achieve mutually desirable goals.

Applying agreed performance

But there is more. Having gone to the trouble to define expectations and gain commitment, the individual somehow has to apply the behaviour agreed to. They have to find a way forward – one that makes it possible for them to actually carry out what they have agreed to do. Yet how often have you found employees in a position where they say they have not been able to put the performance they have agreed into practice? Why do you think this happens?

When you engage in performance counselling it is desirable that you check out with each person how likely it is that they can put into practice what you have both agreed. If you don't you will have created the illusion that all is well and going ahead, when instead you have created an additional problem. It is therefore imperative that you consider the factors which may act to block or inhibit the person putting in the agreed performance. You need to ask yourself a number of critical questions. Has this person got what it takes to produce the performance we have decided and agreed? Have they got the necessary skills and competence? Are we clear about what we mean by performance and the form it will take? What results do we expect to see, hear, observe, find or can be recorded that will give us a clear indication that the agreed performance is being carried through into action?

You should also ask yourself the bigger, but often ignored, question: is this person in the job best suited to them? If not, they will not make the most of themselves and their contribution may be mediocre, not because they are demotivated, unenthusiastic or disagreeable but simply because they are in the wrong job.

Matching people to the jobs required to be done is vital. Yet we need to get much better at it if we are to reduce the view that some 66 per cent of people are in the wrong job, or at least jobs for which they are unsuited. Meredith Belbin, the international organizational consultant, has also wondered why 'in every organization at least one person is in the wrong job'.

When you practise performance counselling you need to make sure you are not pressing people into performances that turn them into misfits in their organization. Misfitting people to the performances we expect of them accounts for many of the failures in goal achievement we set with each other. Apart from that it is a recipe for personal misery, demotivation and job dissatisfaction.

Reviewing results – facts and feelings

In *Hard Times,* Charles Dickens' character Mr Gradgrind tries to sum up what reviewing results are in performance counselling. He says 'Now what I want is, facts. Facts alone are wanted in life.' We don't have to agree that life is made up only of facts, but in performance counselling you do need to know the facts. You need to know what results you are reviewing and whether these were the intended goals you set in the earlier stages of performance counselling. You need to know if the performances of employees have achieved results you never set out to achieve. And you need to know if the results they have achieved were due to the performances they carried through into action. Above all you need to be clear about what counts as a result.

But facts alone are not enough when you are reviewing performance with others. You also have to be aware of *artefacts*. An artefact arises out of a situation where, regardless of the performance put in by people, you would have achieved or failed to achieve the goals you set. The boom in the sales of houses in the UK in the mid-1980s could have been attributed to great sales performance by estate agents. But then the interest rate soared. The result: house sales fell dramatically. The sales executives were still trying to sell, perhaps even harder than before, but sales still dropped. A clear-cut case of an artefact in action. Sales of houses were much more influenced by the level of interest and mortgage lending rates than sales performance. So take care when you are reviewing performance with people. Give them credit where credit is due. Prize them for their efforts – but be critical. Be careful you are not attributing results to performance of others when you need to attribute results to artefacts in your organization, the market or the economy.

On top of this, remember that people matter. Organizational behaviour – your organization – is made up of the aggregate of human behaviour, and as human beings we all have feelings. Reviewing results in performance counselling is as much about feelings as facts – your feelings and the feelings of employees. Feelings are not as easy to specify and measure as facts, but it is salutory to remember that 'not everything that counts is countable and not everything that is countable counts'.

What matters in performance counselling is the whole person and their performance – not just some isolated set of facts. The person is their performance. Don't forget it: if you do, you run the risk of treating performance counselling with people as if they were machines. When you are finding out the facts, you need to ask how people feel about the results you are discussing with them; and when you are talking about their feelings find out if there are any facts to back up what they say. Both facts and feelings are involved in reviewing results in performance counselling: without feelings we are only half human; without facts we cannot know if we are efficient.

Assignment 1

Hygiene and motivator key

Earlier in this chapter you were asked to complete a motivational scale. It consisted of Hygiene and Motivator factors. Use the key below to score you results; H = hygiene factor and M = motivator factor and the numbers beside them represent the questions from the scale.

Hygiene factors: H-2, H-3, H-4, H-5, H-7, H-10, H-13.
Motivators: M-1, M-6, M-8, M-9, M-11, M-12, M-14, M-15.

- How well did you do?
- What is your pattern of motivation?
- What does it mean to you?
- What is the pattern of motivation for people at work?
- What does it mean to them? How do you know?
- How can the motivation of people at work be maintained?
- How can it be improved?
- Does the design of the job need to change or the person in the job?

Personal motivation analyses

Clearly we need to know what motivates people in their work. Complete this analysis yourself and with those who can benefit from performance counselling at work:

- What motivates me most is:

  ✍...
- I attend work because:

  ✍...

- I like my work because:

  ✍...
- The best thing about my work is:

  ✍...
- The worst thing about my work is:

  ✍...
- I can tell I am having a 'bad' day at work because:

  ✍...
- I find I am having a 'good' day at work when:

  ✍...
- A change I would like to make that would motivate me more is:

  ✍...

Assignment 2

- What policy do you have in your organization for growing your own people?
- Where is it working and breaking down?
- Meet with your team and find out what their growth and development needs are.

The green-fingered manager

How green-fingered are you? Do you have the essential attitudes that make you a green-fingered manager? Complete this self-assessment section and discuss the results with your colleagues, subordinates or superiors. How far do they see you the way you see yourself? Why? Why not?

- I listen carefully to people before giving my
  opinion   True/False
- I show my interest in other people's feelings   True/False
- I work things out together with people   True/False
- I am clear in my communication with others   True/False
- I never jump to conclusions   True/False
- I don't think people are weak if they have
  problems   True/False

• People are able to share their aspirations and ambitions with me	True/False
• People feel safe with me	True/False
• I encourage people to do their best	True/False
• I bring out the best in people	True/False
• People think I am tough with them	True/False
• People believe I care about them	True/False
• I work out with people the best course of action	True/False
• I review how well people are performing with them and get their views	True/False
• I am as interested in people as in the tasks/ goals we set	True/False

Meet with your colleagues, work group or team and share and compare your results. How do you see yourself? Do the others agree? What perspectives need to be changed? Which ones should you maintain and continue to develop? Build a personal learning agenda for yourself to increase your competence and skills as a green-fingered manager.

2

THE POWER OF RELATIONSHIPS

'The most important principles that managers should apply are to know themselves, improve people skills, talk with instead of to subordinates, avoid stereotyping them, and be sensitive to what they want out of their work.' *Jones and Woodcock*

Building strength through trust

Why is it some managers bring out the best in people and others just seem to be pushing and pulling without getting anywhere? You only have to listen to any informal gathering of managers to get a ready clue. Among an animated exchange you may have heard these well-rehearsed epithets: 'I keep pushing my people – you've got to stay on their tails'; 'I can't trust them to get on with it'; 'The main problem is they don't trust me and I don't trust them'. Sound familiar? Employees are not going to perform well and neither are we if we don't have a good working relationship at work. Essential to this is the need to trust each other. If we don't trust each other, there is the risk of creating Julius Caesar managers who are suspicious of their employees and never trust them – managers who think and believe that everyone around them is dangerous and 'has a lean and hungry look'. Such an atmosphere at work prevents getting at the real issues and problems people are trying to solve. It also blocks the achievement of personal and organizational goals.

Without trust, you maintain a climate of fear, and where there is fear there is little risk-taking. Yet risk-taking is what often makes employees buzz with excitement and ideas. It is risk-taking that separates the mountain-climbers from the footpath walkers. Risk-taking is essential for the success of modern organizations. As a Malaysian proverb puts it: 'As the drum beats, so goes the dance.'

The first big step towards effective performance counselling is to develop a deep and lasting sense of trust amongst employees and managers alike. So how can managers establish a climate of trust at work between themselves and the employees? Trust is the bread of communication: it can only be enjoyed once we have achieved a sense of safety and security with the persons we work with and the environment in which work is carried out.

Rule number one then in developing trust is: *create a climate of safety and security with employees.* This trust-building climate should concentrate on the psychological aspects of safety and security as much as the physical ones. To build trust involves a risk: the risk of sharing yourself. This means disclosing some of yourself to your employees; it means showing them that you are a person, and in turn employees will show themselves to you. It means being able to change things by first of all changing yourself. Managers who can do this begin to demonstrate to employees that it is safe to do so.

Personal power

Personal power is not the kind you force on others or make them conform to and comply with. The actions we take, and influence we have as a result of those actions, tell us how much personal power we exert at any particular time, in specific situations with each person. Warren Bennis and Burt Nanus declared in their best-selling book *Leaders:* 'Power is the basic energy to initiate and sustain action translating intention into reality, the quality without which leaders cannot lead.'

The personal power found in relationship-building is one which is directed towards freeing the competencies and abilities of employees. It is the ethical use of personal power and trust is the fuel that drives it. When Christ said 'Follow me' he was using personal power. People were driven to follow him because they trusted him.

When people feel safe and secure they are motivated to solve their problems. They trust you. They will move mountains for you. However, trust is a two-way track. If you prove to be untrustworthy, then the consequences of the lack of trust will come tumbling down like a pack of playing cards. Long ago Shakespeare reminded us in *Henry VI* that we should 'Trust not him that hath once broken faith'. Misplaced trust, when revealed, is worse than not having trusted a person in the first place. What is needed is mutual respect. Without mutual respect – without shared trustworthiness – managers and employees will have a rough ride, and the manager who has responsibility for empowering employees to overcome their difficulties and work-related problems is, in a word, going to be unsuccessful. Since managers were expected to manage it is they who must be the first to initiate trust and build it up with employees. If you don't risk yourself with others, they will not risk themselves with you.

Role models – breakdown or breakthrough

Right from birth we are faced with role models: the people we see around us, our parents, relatives, and friends. Their behaviours are the ones we copy: 'He is just like his father or mother', 'She does exactly the same as you', 'He learned to be like that by watching his brother'.

Role models provide the learning templates for us to copy. Why do we do it? Because it is rewarding – but not all role models are useful for growing people and enabling them to use the skills and competencies they have to solve their problems and develop new and desirable behaviours. The riots at Strangeways prison in Manchester lasted 25 days and received marathon media coverage. Television provides a vast and diverse range of role models. Strangeways received lots of attention and high-profile reporting. Soon after the initial rioting, copycat riots started to break out in other prisons. A clear case of role modelling the riot behaviour of the prisoners in Strangeways. On the other hand, the achievements of Nick Faldo in winning the Masters golf championship 'back-to-back' resulted in a rush of 'Faldo type' golfers wanting to copy his style. Sales of the golfing tapes and equipment used by Faldo no doubt increased rapidly. Sponsors know the profit value of high-profile role models.

There is a meaningful message here for organizations and managers who wish to grow their own people. Adopting role models can be the basis for a breakthrough into personal growth or a breakdown of individuals in organizations and what they are trying to achieve. It is important that you know which role models in your organization are being sponsored and which are not. When you do know, employees will have a powerful key to avoiding breakdown and facilitating the breakthrough to new and productive behaviour.

It is a key question managers in organizations need to ask themselves seriously. One executive from a large oil company I knew summed up the dilemma for people in his organization. He said: 'Here they ask you to do things one way but when you see what people do on the ground it is completely different.' For people to grow in their capacities to solve their own problems and to contribute to their organization they need to know which role models are rewarded and which are discouraged or penalized. If you want people to grow, first of all check out the role models you are really promoting at work. If they are ones that lead to staleness, frustration and foul-ups, you need to change them. Such role models are a menace to the further growth of individual employees and are dangerous for the future of the organization. When you detect role models that you want to encourage, give people the opportunity to link with them. When you provide appropriate role models for growth and development you also increase the likelihood of personal success and rewarding work. One way to confirm this is to observe and talk to people in a part of your organization that is working well and where they are dealing effectively with their personal problems. You can safely bet you will find the role models provided there play a large part in its success.

Nurturing for personal growth

Getting started with the right role models does something else: it helps to prepare the soil for the nurturing and personal growth of employees. Without this nurturing you will not get growth in the individual. You might get a brief show of forced enthusiasm and shallow commitment – a five-minute wonder. To overcome this kind of frustrating short-termism it is nurturing that is required.

The reason nurturing people is important is that they are not just bodies doing work. As Alfred Adler said: 'There can no longer be any doubt that everything we call a body shows a striving to become a whole.' Nurturing provides the soil for becoming the competent and complete person many employees want to be. Treating people like numbers in a box or just 'another pair of hands' – a phrase commonly used in nursing and other large organizations – chokes off nurturing. The consequences of failing to nurture people is death – death of effort, death of interest, death of motivation, death of job-satisfaction and death of any significant contribution to their employing organizations. Where you have these characteristics, someone, somewhere in your organization, is suffering through lack of nurturing. Tom Peters, guru of people and organizations, recommends getting out of the office and managing by 'wandering about' among your employees. Try asking them how well supported they are. In some cases you will see the slow lingering death that is evidenced through the lack of nurturing.

Personal problems multiply when nurturing is absent, but they are faced and tackled with courage by people when nurturing is present. Which do you prefer? Nurturing wins every time. It breeds courage – the kind of courage that enables people to face up to their personal problems and change in organizations.

Nurturing is not a soft option or easy ride. It is not an excuse for avoiding solving personal and work-related problems. So what is nurturing? Nurturing is the essential provision of caring in an organization. Charles Handy has observed how necessary caring for the nurturing of people in organizations must become: 'Care is not a word to be found in many organizational textbooks... but it should be. Forgiveness is not easy without unconditional positive regard of the sort we feel for our children, no matter how much we disapprove of their behaviour. People do not take risks with those they do not trust or genuinely care for.' Subsidiarity comes from more of that trust and more of that positive regard. Loose, dispersed organizations depend on people liking and trusting each other. A culture of question and experiment, of exploration and adventure, cannot survive a reign of fear. That kind of culture cannot be imposed; it can only be encouraged by demonstrations of warmth for all that is good, by celebration, by investment in individuals beyond the bounds of prudence. That kind of encouragement is only possible if one genuinely cares for the people being encouraged.'

Managers who can create a genuine climate of care and nurturing at work take a giant step forwards in their thinking, their values and the way they manage human resources. To create a climate of care at work you need to know about caring. Caring is the basis of nurturing. Caring is based on what I call 'The Triple A Factor'. The Triple A Factor of nurturing means being able to convey to people at work a sense of

- Affiliation
- Association
- Affection.

Affiliation

Affiliation is key to nurturing because we all need to affiliate with others. Some people have higher affiliation needs than others. Nonetheless, the need for affiliations must be acknowledged if nurturing is to occur. Work, social and sports clubs, professional associations and religious societies are all traditional and established ways of affiliating with other people. It is often said that those nurses who are good at recognizing affiliation needs are popular with patients – and sales personnel who are the same are likely to be popular with their customers. On a more day-to-day level, the British pub, continental cafe and American soda fountain and hamburger bar are all typical expressions of the way people show their need to affiliate with each other. Affiliation says we are members, we belong, we identify with each other. Affiliation at work contributes to the nurturing of people, how good they feel about themselves and the organization within which they work. The absence of affiliation opportunities either at or outside of work can raise problems for people, their health and performance. Failure to satisfy the affiliation needs of people makes them restless, irritable and discontented. In some extreme cases, failure to affiliate may result in severe depression. Not every loner 'wants to be alone'. So look out for the ways you can open up affiliation opportunities for people at work.

Association

Affiliation provides the basis for association between people at work and outside work. Being able to associate with others builds the bridges necessary for caring and nurturing people at work. When you think of it, association tells us a lot about people and how we treat them. Given freedom of choice, people choose who they wish to associate with, who their friends will be and how they associate with them. Unfortunately, freedom to associate can also be influenced by other factors outside the control of employees. Sometimes the section, office, department, factory, depot or store they work in already prescribes who they will largely associate with at work. However, within the confines of a group of employees selective association can go on informally. People seek each other out, become friends or acquaintances, and establish different degrees of social intimacy.

The caring organization is sensitive to the association needs of its employees. It does not wittingly or unwittingly create problems for its employees. However, there are examples of organizations that have moved people around, to different parts of the organization or to different parts of the country – or even to overseas locations – without sufficient consideration to their needs for association with others. Associating with others in the organization gives people a sense of cohesion, a way of maintaining and developing social networks at work. Take them away or exclude people from associating with each other and what happens? You get trouble. Separate dining areas, toilets, travelling facilities, and privileges inhibit the growth of people. They create organizational apartheid.

If you want to facilitate the growth of people don't create division. Division is a formula for frustration, conflict, discontent and suspicion. Managers who have to deal with suspicion face a long and lonely uphill struggle. What is the alternative? We have to reverse organizational patterns and practices that inhibit the personal growth and development of people at work. Some of these adverse work patterns have been created over months and often years. Facilitating association at work strengthens people. It generates cells of cohesive people networks that can sustain and support each other at times of personal difficulties and celebrate their triumphs, victories and successes.

Affection

'Everybody needs somebody – sometime' – so the song goes; and it's a fact. Being able to affiliate with others and associating with chosen people allow the expression of affection. Being able to express affection to employees says to them: You count – you are important. Too many firms concentrate on headcounting, number-crunching and cash accounting at the expense of showing affection to their employees. You will not get far by remembering finance and forgetting people – both count.

Managers need to convey affection clearly to their people. As Will Shutz, the American psychologist, knew we need to receive affection from others as well as giving it to them. Giving and receiving affection openly feeds people. It tells them you are more than a number; you are not just a body – a machine. You are a person with feelings and beliefs and I am a person with feelings and beliefs as well.

Denying the need to give and receive affection at work creates problems for people, their growth and their performance. When we rob people of our affections we short-change them. And when we are short-changed in return we start cutting off the human face of work. When this happens people stop having fun – work should be fun for people.

When people feel affection and give it in return work becomes less effort. As Mark Twain once said: 'Fun is what you do when you don't have to do it.' Finding work fun is a sure sign that affection is being shared with others. It doesn't just depend on the tasks that are being done. Work tasks can still be unpleasant and frustrating to carry out, but the reward lies in the sharing of affection and the message that people 'belong' – they are recognized, they count. If you want to help people with problems of personal growth in your organization take a tip from Bill Glasser, the advocate of reality counselling. 'What I am almost always strongly aware of is that I want to belong. I want to be part of a group, maybe of many groups. There are times when I want to be alone, but I never want to be lonely. Even when I am by myself and temporarily satisfied, I want to know that if I reach out, someone is there.'

Belonging versus disempowerment

Just being in an organization can be enough to generate disempowerment for many employees. As Rudolph Moos, the American psychologist, has demonstrated, each organization has its own social climate. If the social climate cultivates and encourages belongingness amongst people, we can expect to feel supported and good about our working relationships, we know what is expected of us and are clear about our roles and goals and the work-based systems and procedures in our organization.

On the other hand, when people feel disempowered, when the social climate creates disempowerment, people feel they do not belong, they are not part of the organization. When people at work believe they do not belong, they lose their sense of purpose. They become alienated from the organization; they sit on the sidelines of work. They become onlookers – observers of events at work – rather than being involved and willing participants in it. When this happens it often goes by unnoticed. As a result, they become aimless and drift along on a sea of resentment and uncertainty – uncertain about their place in the organization or the work they do, uncertain about their value or their contribution to the enterprise. How many people in your organization feel or think this way? None, some, many? If you don't know the answer then you have a belongingness problem in your organization.

In its extreme form, a lack of employee identity or belongingness can produce a profound sense of alienation and sense of separation from the organization. People often fail to identify with the organization because it has failed to identify with them. Lack of appropriate participation in decision-making between managers and employees is a classic example that leads to separation and alienation at work.

Managers play a large part in creating or breaking a sense of belonging for people at work. Not every manager gets it wrong – many get it right. They encourage people to belong and share in a common vision and purpose, as well as creating choices for social cohesion and a strong sense of being personally valued for the work they do. Their contribution is deliberately and consciously recognized. These green-fingered managers make it their business to let employees know how important they are to the business and its success. The payoff for the manager is a workforce with a strong sense of corporate cohesion, high morale and company loyalty.

Belongingness and a sense of shared purpose go hand in hand. They should also be highly visible to others inside and outside the organization. They are a statement of people empowerment at work. You only need to look around some organizations to sense and see a strong presence of shared identity and belongingness. Companies like McDonalds, Burger King, John Lewis, Shell, BP, Marks and Spencer, British Telecom, Johnson and Johnson, Pedigree Petfoods and Mars Confectionery are all high-visibility organizations that convey a strong sense of employee belongingness at work. Green-fingered managers know that belongingness inspires fresh ideas, self-esteem, risk-taking and commitment to the organization and its objectives.

Belongingness and self-esteem

People can feel they belong in their organization and still have low self-esteem. Conversely, they can have high self-esteem and not feel they belong. When this happens, they are getting their self-esteem from outside work but don't feel they identify with their organization. The critical factor is to empower people to enjoy self-esteem at work *and* still feel a strong sense of belongingness in their organization.

To belong, people must feel they belong. Managers can facilitate or inhibit belonging, and the green-fingered manager understands how important it is for employees to feel they belong and identify with their organization. Practical performance counselling means being able to reach out to others to give them a signal – the signal that gives them the starting point to reach back to you. When you can do this you have a sound foundation on which to get started in counselling.

Not belonging, alienation and stress at work

Not belonging can be extremely stressful for employees and can result in unnecessary stress and personal alienation – a formula that produces loners and outsiders inside organizations. Clearly, this is bad news: it is bad for the health, well-being and happiness of employees; it is also bad for the productive performance of organizations. Organizations that have a poor social climate – especially where belongingness and self-esteem is low and alienation high – are underperforming organizations. They are likely to suffer from low morale, high staff turnover and high absence from work.

The stress produced through alienation can become very serious indeed for some employees. Emile Durkheim, in his work *Suicide,* observed how extreme forms of alienation in organizations and society at large can lead to people taking their own lives. Clearly, where there is a marked absence of a sense of belonging, no shared purpose, no involvement in making decisions and a dearth of mutual affiliation, association or affection, employees are going to experience dissatisfaction with their work and their motivation to work will be severely tested. As if this was not enough, such people are also likely to increase their vulnerability to sickness and absence from work. Sometimes they may experience a crisis of confidence and require crisis counselling for the personal stress that has been induced through the lack of caring in the organization. At these times, the green-fingered manager reaches out to support people at work.

Pacing in empowering others

It is important not to get off to a false start. You need to avoid getting stuck at the starting gate. Getting started in performance counselling is a bit like a racehorse and its rider. They need to pace each other. Rushing headlong for the first fence can end in disaster for rider and horse. And using all of your energy in the first few lengths gives you little reserve on which to draw in the final furlong of the race.

In performance counselling you need to pace the person you have reached out to, or has asked you for help. Like the jockey on the horse you need to control the energy and enable people to make the most of the choices available to them. The horse and jockey combine the rider's competence with the capabilities of the horse. In practising performance counselling you pace yourself with the person or group. The specific skills that get you well away from the starting post are 'matching' and 'mirroring'.

Matching and mirroring

Matching involves sharing the emblems, symbols and behaviour that make us comfortable with others and willing to work with them. Emblems can range all the way from company ties and suits through to the kind of office you are allocated according to seniority in the organization. Symbols are more emphatic than emblems. Symbols are visual statements about a person and their organization. When someone writes to you on headed paper with Shell printed on it they are making a statement about themselves. It says 'I line up with this organization'. It also says 'This organization lines itself up with me'. This is a match. In performance counselling, you need to be conscious of matching yourself well with individuals. Wear different emblems, convey different symbols, and you get a mismatch.

Mismatching can create communication blocks between people. The Japanese in their single-status organizations have deliberately avoided mismatching between emblems and symbols among their personnel. This is one reason why Toyota, Nissan and Mitsubishi are so part of our consciousness. The same can be said in the USA for IBM, Coca-Cola, Pepsi, General Motors, Ford and McDonalds. In Europe, Pedigree Petfoods and Mars Confectionery are excellent examples of single-status companies sharing the same emblems, symbols and behaviour. These organizations realize the importance of good pacing through matchmaking.

Avoiding mismatching in performance counselling

When someone needs performance counselling make sure you are not setting up a mismatch: it creates unnecessary and irrelevant side-tracking. Mismatching in performance counselling is not just limited to dress and position in the organization; it can also come from the language used by white-collar and blue-collar workers. So in counselling employees match up, rather than mismatch.

When you are able to get suitable matching you need to sustain it. This is usually done by mirroring your conversations and actions with others. Probably the most literal example of mirroring is the children's game of sidling up alongside a glass store window and waving their legs up and down so that they look as if they are flying. The illusion is created by using the reflections of the window to mirror our movements back to us. However, mirroring is not straightforward copying. It is more like a dance with complementary movements in action and the way people behave and talk with each other. Mirroring can and should be very subtle and not crude or rude.

When in performance counselling a person may say: 'I'm frustrated with so little progress on this project.' Your counselling reply could be: 'You feel like you're hitting your head against a brick wall.' Mirroring is also about reflecting back to a person that they have been heard. When they know they have been heard, they can share with you what it is that is worrying them, annoying them, thrilling them, or just simply what's 'on their mind'. It is irritating and downright unhelpful when a person doesn't know that they are being understood. Altogether, it's a waste of time and time is money. When a person says to you, 'I can't face going to the office today', you don't say, 'You'd better get right down there because Phillips will be gunning for you if you don't.' That isn't mirroring. It's threats and fear. Above all, it's poor managing. The manager using mirroring could make a big difference in this example. A typical mirroring reply would be: 'There seems to be something about going to the office that you really want to avoid today.'

Why mirror? Well for a start mirroring offers people the opportunity to say what is on their mind. On top of this, it permits you to avoid making gross and often inaccurate assumptions about why people say and do what they do. If you want to give people the chance to grow, then use matching and mirroring. It is a powerful personal relationship-building approach to people.

Reading the face

Matching and mirroring can be used in conversation and in the expressions we signal back and forth to each other. But matching and mirroring alone are not enough. We also need to be able to read the face. The thousands of communications that are shown on our faces each minute are not always easily comprehended unless we make a point of practising it.

In their book *Unmasking the Face*, Eckman and Friesen showed how we tend to use a number of standard expressions that are important for others to be able to read. If we are unable to read another's facial expressions accurately we run the risk of becoming face-illiterate – a situation where we don't understand people and they don't understand our not being able to understand them.

Interestingly, few people seem to be able to read another person's face very well. Apart from knowing when a person is happy, managers need to know when others are angry, confused, surprised or in fear of situations at work, and fear is at the basis of many failed work initiatives. Where there is fear there is no risk-taking. So get clued up on reading the faces of people. Try checking it out with them and see how well you do, but don't be surprised to find out that to begin with you get it wrong. Find out from your people what they look like when they are unhappy; what expressions they have when they don't understand what it is they are supposed to do; and get to know how you can help them overcome their fear of taking risks for themselves and their company.

Assignment

Belongingness survey – do you belong?

Our feeling of the degree of belongingness in an organization affects our motivation, level of personal stress, job satisfaction, and how closely we identify with our colleagues. Completing this belongingness survey will help to focus on the sense of belongingness or separation experienced in an organization. Complete the survey questions as quickly as possible. When you have done this, consider what the results mean to you and discuss them with your colleagues, manager or company counsellor. Decide which answers apply to you right now and record them in each box using this system of marking:

1 = never   2 = rarely   3 = sometimes   4 = often   5 = always

  1 I feel people at my place of work are my sort of people ....[ ]
  2 At work I am involved in the things that matter ....[ ]
  3 I actively contribute to my group or work team ....[ ]
  4 I believe the work I do is appreciated.............................[ ]
  5 I feel close to many of the people I work with ....[ ]
  6 I know my boss cares about what I think and feel ....[ ]
  7 This organization listens to what its employees have to say ....[ ]
  8 I control important aspects of my job...............................[ ]
  9 I feel part of my job ....[ ]
10 I feel proud of the work I do ....[ ]

Scoring guide

Up to 20

People who score in this range tend to feel isolated at work and separated from their organization. Their personal stress is likely to be high. They may even feel depressed, demotivated and uninterested in their work. They are also probably unhappy and underperforming at work. You should listen to what they have to say and provide them with expert help soon.

21-30

People who score in this range may have a cycle of good days and bad days at work – but it is likely they will have more good days than bad. They don't feel completely out of the mainstream of the organization; however, they don't feel part of what is going on either – to any great degree. They are not outsiders but stand on the sidelines of the organization. Work out how you can take more interest in what they do.

31-40

If people have any of these scores, it suggests they do have a sense of belonging and feeling of importance in the organization. Most of the time, they will feel that they are valued for their contribution to the organization and that it cares for them. They will tend to have a strong sense of belongingness in their organization. They are also likely to be representative of the majority of employees unless the organization is going through a period of rapid and uncertain change. If this is the case, you can expect the percentage of people in this category to decrease and move more towards feelings of discomfort, separation and alienation.

41-50

People with scores in this range are those who are at present loyal and completely dedicated to the organization. It has become part of them. Without a doubt, they belong – it is their organization. They have no problems of separation or alienation from the organization. Instead they have a deep and abiding sense of belonging. Problems of belonging and separation are likely to occur only if rumours start of redundancy or other threats to their identity and position in the organization.

Assignment

Matching and mirroring are part of every organization. Matching and mirroring can be seen in the kinds of clothes we wear, the cars we drive, the places we eat and the kinds of conversations and interests we share. The way people match and mirror each other is an indicator of how much they like each other and who they align with. It is also a signal that people are willing to identify with you. Map out who identifies with you and who you identify with in your organization/department/office. What are the benefits of matching and mirroring? What are the drawbacks of mismatching with colleagues/superiors/subordinates? How will you put any mismatching or unsatisfactory mirroring right?

Personal action to improve matching/mirroring

✍ ....

....

....

....

....

....

....

....

....

3

OVERCOMING BARRIERS TO CHANGE

'Those who wear pearls do not know how many times the diver
has been bitten by the sharks.' *Ethiopian proverb*

Approaching the hurdles of change

Building relationships with people at work provides the solid ground-
work for effective performance counselling. It gives us the
foundations for working with people, their performances, and achieving real change – change that they want and we want.

What could be simpler? However, more has to be done before the
real and lasting effects of performance counselling can be seen in
employees and their performance at work. The main hurdle managers
have to cross in preparing themselves to carry out performance counselling is to recognize the need for employees to defend themselves
against any change. Simply forcing individuals to agree with you and
state their problems, goals and aspirations will achieve very little.
Like the horse, you will have led it to water but it will not drink –
even though it is parched and dying of thirst. Why? Because, not only
does the horse have to trust you, it has to want to drink and it has to
know that it is worth the risk of drinking the water in the first place.

Performance counselling is like that. Drag the person to your point
of view and you get nowhere. People are usually highly guarded when
'counselled' in this way. They defend themselves and are not prepared
to open up and explore the real issues affecting them and their performance. A bit like pearl-divers: they have been bitten too often for
taking risks. You have to be sensitive to their hurts as well as their

possibilities. To me this is the key to performance counselling and managers should be aware of it. When you are conducting performance counselling you are asking people to take risks. They need to know they are not going to get bitten – and not suffer deeply as a result of diving for their pearls. The pearls are the personal and untapped resources inside everyone. To discover and release them you need to know the most common defence mechanisms that people use to cover up their pearls. These defence mechanisms are the barriers to change that need to be understood and overcome for us to achieve real and lasting change in individuals and their performance.

Common defence mechanisms

Denial
Refusing to accept or perceive a shared reality.

Examples: Pretending you are not stunned, hurt or angry when you are told you are being made redundant. Not letting other employees see that you are annoyed with their shabby treatment of customers. Refusing to acknowledge errors or take responsibility for overspend in departmental budgets.

Fantasy
Imagining achievements that have no factual grounds.

Example: Telling people you are being promoted to head up your organization – claiming customers you don't have – giving pay rises you can't afford.

Rationalization
Attempting to prove that actions are 'rational' and justifiable to gain approval or acceptance from others.

Example: Simms had to be demoted 'in the interests' of all concerned – giving better offices to managers on the basis that they need them 'because of the work they do'.

Projection
Blaming others for our own mistakes or attributing our own unethical desires to others.

Example: The project would have succeeded if planning did not mess up the detail – Thomson will have to stop trying to have his own way all of the time.

Reaction formulation
Preventing the expression of dangerous desires or emotions by exaggerating and claiming the opposite attitudes and behaviour.

Example: I like Williams very much and he is such a great man to have in the team – I would never think of leaking our organization's financial position to others.

Emotional insulation
Reducing our personal ego involvement with others to protect ourselves and avoid getting hurt.

Example: I know Jill has given me 100 per cent support over the years and now she is totally against me – but managers like her are 'ten a penny' – Sheila's drink problem has ruined the figures for this set of accounts but that has nothing to with me.

Displacement
Discharging pent-up feelings – usually hostility – on to things or people who are less threatening and were not the source of danger.

Example: That's right, Witherspoon, make a bloody mess of making the coffee! Can't you do anything right! (middle manager to office junior after being heavily criticized and disciplined by a meeting of senior managers).

Intellectualization
Suppressing the emotional aspect of hurtful situations and separating incompatible attitudes through 'logic tight' compartments.

Example: The divorce had to come – we were never suited to each other in the first place – work is work and home-life is home-life.

Compensation
Covering up weaknesses by emphasizing some other desirable quality or attitude or making up for frustration or disappointment in one area of life by overgratifying in another.

Example: I know I don't have the competence to lead this team but what this team really needs is loyalty and you know, John, there is nobody more loyal than me – ever since the marriage broke up six months ago she/he has been on a non-stop spending spree.

Acting out
The reduction of anxiety or other stressful emotions by permitting and engaging in their expression.

Example: OK, so I got angry at the meeting and went on like that for a full hour and a half. I don't know if it made any sense to the team – but I felt a whole lot better.

Defensive routines

Chris Argyris, Professor of Education and Organizational behaviour at Harvard, claims that these defences can also act as defensive routines. They are the anchors that make our behaviour solid and stable. We need them. Why? Because they stand us in good stead to manage our personal and working lives. But only up to a point.

Defensive routines work in many situations. For example, when we are brought bad news we can use our defensive routines to help us protect ourselves and to find new ways of coping with the situation. If sales executives broke down every time they did not get an order or lost a customer, they would be unable to look after their other customers or get fresh orders for their company. In a situation like this, the sales executive can go into a defensive routine. Rationalization and intellectualization would help to give him or her sufficient stability to 'think' and work out what went wrong, and how to put things right, or whether to bother at all spending time pursuing the recovery of the account.

Defensive routines can be productive and counterproductive for individuals and the organizations within which they work. However, adopting them over long periods of time can have disastrous effects. A good example of defensive routines is the way hospitals encourage nurses to behave. Have you ever noticed how well they safeguard themselves against anxiety when they have to treat patients? The health services researcher Isobel Menzies was the first observer to record how nurses are encouraged by the hospital organization not to 'see people in pain who need help'. Instead, the organization adopted, encouraged and supported nurses in a defensive strategy. They were asked to treat (1) a patient, with (2) a diagnosis and (3) a number in

(4) a bed with (5) an illness. A very powerful defensive strategy which nurses were expected to adopt as their own defensive routine.

However, this use of defensive routines only proves productive up to a point. It allows nurses and doctors to perform the acts of healing and helping without experiencing disabling levels of stress and anxiety. But these defensive routines also prevent real change happening: change that may be desired by the individuals receiving treatment and those engaged in the process of their recovery. It has since been discovered that giving patients more information and control over their stay in hospital and their participation in their treatment decisions, facilitates the rate at which they recover. The same processes hold good for the practice of performance counselling in commercial companies and other public service organizations.

Productive and counterproductive routines

You can start the process now by asking how productive and counterproductive defensive routines are for you, your employees and your organization. Which ones does your organization encourage or disapprove of? The downside of defensive routines is that they provide the concrete that sets our habits and prevents genuine personal and organizational change. Personal and organizational change can be threatening and when it is, we tend to engage in various defensive routines to resist the very changes we say we want to create. Defensive routines allow us to say one thing and do another, and this poses a problem when we are working with people who need to change their way of managing their problems and their performances. The more defended a person is, the less real change you will get from them. In these situations you can expect a number of different responses when they are engaged in performance counselling. First, they may not 'see the need' for change in themselves or what they are doing. These people are so well defended it is like trying to dismantle Edinburgh Castle with a toothpick. It hurts you more than it hurts them and you make little impression on them and they know it.

Another way people respond is by expressing the Abilene Paradox. Here you find that the person agrees with you the kinds of things they want to change and how they will go about making changes in their behaviour and performance at work. The only trouble is – and this is the paradox – they carry on in the same way as they did before. No change.

The third possibility, and you hope it is the one that works, is that people are motivated and find the resources in themselves to make the changes agreed with you in the counselling session. Wouldn't it be nice if life was so simple? If all we read in management development books and counselling were so simple to apply, we would all be experts in developing others and increasing their personal performance. But when performance counselling at work is taken seriously and managers know how to use and refine their counselling skills they *can* help people to improve their performance significantly. One of the big secrets in counselling is to work with the grain of each individual and not against them.

Utilizing defensive routines

Initially it helps to utilize people's defensive routines. Simply pulling them apart or insisting that they should 'stop being defensive' makes you an expert in one thing – in making people defensive. You are saying, 'Hey, you know those defensive routines you are using, the ones that have worked for you so long – stop using them!'

The first tenet of good performance counselling as we are using it in this book is simple. Get close to people and make it *safe* for them to get close to you. Insisting on others dropping their defensive routines pulls away the safety net of defensive routines. It says trust me – right away. How many times have you been able to do this yourself? Go on, tell me. You are the trusting type. That's a great defensive routine. Asking for trust right away and expecting to get it without preparing the ground for a growing relationship – the basis of performance counselling – is like asking a person to drive a car without a steering wheel.

Some managers think 'Oh well, if you are unable to get rid of your defensive routines, let me do it for you.' They then proceed to use various questionable, debatable and dubious means to 'help' the person get rid of their defences. Sometimes this is done in a 'counselling session' – a session that amounts to a kind of tribal barbarism where you must reveal and confess your all to me, and more. The session has to be completed in 15 minutes because that's all the time the manager has available. Here's an example.

The computer printer – a case of defensive routines in action

Engaging in defensive routines and failing to create the conditions for change can be a great cost to individuals and their companies. One company specialising in high-quality commercial computer printers was going through a period of rapid change and losing market share to its competitors. After a series of urgent meetings it was decided that the company should enter the personal computer market with a new printer suitable for the PC market, a cheap and high-volume product. The senior managers believed that introducing a new but cheaper and less high-quality printer to the PC market would help return their market share. The idea and the decision seemed sound. They anticipated the results would be high-volume sales for the company. To do this meant involving the technical team in the acceptance of the idea and obtaining their commitment to the success of the project. The time span between the concept for the PC and availability of the new printer was set at six months. Sales promotion was to start right away.

Much depended upon the marketing manager creating the conditions where the head of technical development would feel part of the decision and want to associate himself and his team with the new computer printer and the deadlines set by the senior managers in the company. Here is a summary of what happened. See if you can notice when the defensive routines are being used and by whom.

Briefing prior to meeting with project manager

Roger Lockhart, the marketing manager, explains to David Mason, sales director – Europe, how he will talk through the project for the new PC printer with Douglas Taylor, the head of technical development.

David. Roger you know it is essential that we get Douglas on board to develop the new PC printer within the six-month deadline we have agreed. At the meeting you said it would not be a problem for marketing and you would speak to Douglas to get his commitment to the project. How do you propose you'll do it?

Roger. I think I know Douglas pretty well by now, David, and I know it is crucial to get his total support for this project. So what I intend to do is this: I will meet with Douglas in his office and tell him how much we have appreciated his work over the years, that whenever we have engaged in new product development he has always supported us, and that I wanted to get his views on a new project we have in mind for a printer suitable for the PC market and the deadlines he would think suitable to get such a project under way and completed by his team.

David. OK, Roger. Now are you sure you will handle it this way and you don't want to spend any more time thinking through about how you will approach Douglas?

Roger. No I am crystal clear on this one, David. In any event, time is of the essence – I must set up the meeting with Douglas right away.

One day later – the meeting with Douglas Taylor

Roger (in his office, speaking in an abrupt manner). Douglas. come in and sit down. I'm glad you could make this urgent meeting at such short notice.

Douglas. You sounded quite urgent on the phone – what is it about?

Roger. I was no more urgent than I usually am – you know me, Douglas, always the first to get ahead and get going... not like you guys round in Technical Development. I haven't got a lot of spare time and that's why I wanted to see you today. You know, I have spoken to you in the past about entering the PC market with one of our own printers... That is what we have decided to do. (Roger denies the urgency of the phone call and starts "talking down" to Douglas Taylor.)

Douglas. I'm sorry Roger, but I don't quite get your drift. What do you mean we have decided. Who?

Roger. The board, Douglas... the board. Everybody is behind it. It is a great leap forward... it will help restore our prominence in the market place. (Roger showing signs of irritation at making an inaccurate and irrational claim about the new printer project.)

Douglas. Nobody consulted me about it. What specific reason was there for...?

Roger. Now look Douglas, the reasons don't matter. We have been through this already... (Roger ignoring Douglas Taylor's need to belong and his request for information and overriding the importance of getting Douglas's views on the project.)

Douglas. Not with me, you haven't. I'm not happy with you suddenly dumping this on me.... I have come all the way round to your office to hear this. It is not on and I am very dubious about a printer in the PC market. It is already saturated with competition. Even if I could be persuaded I doubt if we would be successful....

Roger. There isn't time for niceties in this, Taylor. The bottom line is we need a new printer for the PC market and we want it ready and on sale in six months. That is the reality, so if you don't cock it up like the Integrated Systems Printer project we might just make it on time. We're counting on you... don't let us down.

Douglas. I've had enough of this meeting, Roger... It has been a waste of my time.

What went wrong?

The meeting went badly wrong from the start. There were a lot of defensive routines at work. First of all Roger Lockhart became defensive when the meeting was held in his own office rather than that of Douglas Taylor. Second, he further indicated his defensiveness by not welcoming Douglas – although he said the words, the tone and meaning in them were highly defensive. Third, he engaged in putting Douglas down and tried to establish his dominance in the meeting.

Fourth, Roger made claims that could not be justified or substantiated. Fifth, Roger did not listen to Douglas Taylor. Sixth he screened out the attempts by Douglas to be heard. Seventh, he failed to acknowledge Douglas's attempts to belong with the people involved in the decision to go ahead with a printer suitable for the PC market. Eighth, Roger did not seek the views of Douglas on the project and how his team might feel about such an undertaking. Ninth, Roger did not let Douglas know how much the board had appreciated the work he had done in the past for the company – especially the urgent projects. Tenth, Roger resorted to blaming Douglas for difficulties they had with the ISP project – a totally irrational and defensive manoeuvre to try to make Douglas feel guilty and induce his motivation to work on the PC printer project.

In summary, Roger Lockhart abandoned the approach he said he would take with Douglas Taylor. Instead he went for a set of defensive routines and manoeuvres intended to manipulate Taylor into agreeing to the project and the deadlines agreed by others. Lockhart settled for creating a defence position where he would be top dog and Taylor would be underdog. But Taylor was not having it.

At the end of this meeting there were a number of outcomes. Roger Lockhart still did not know Douglas Taylor's views on the PC project. Taylor did not feel he belonged in the project. He and Lockhart did not establish a rapport. This created further problems at their future meetings. The new PC was eventually produced. It took two years. The company missed an opportunity: it entered an already busy market with its new product. It is difficult to estimate but it probably cost them millions. It did not increase their market share.

This case demonstrates clearly the difference between an espoused theory of empowering others and the theory in use or that put into action by Roger Lockhart. The outcomes would have been very different if Lockhart could have put into practice his espoused theory of how he would approach Douglas Taylor. Just how much, we can only guess; the chances are the PC printer would have been ready and on the market within 12 months – maybe even the six-month deadline set by the original product development meeting. Lockhart and Taylor would have had rapport, respect and trust and they would be listening to each other. Taylor would probably be much more motivated at work and have a strong sense of belonging in the company and in his relationship with Lockhart. Above all. Lockhart, Taylor and the other managers in the company would have learned a powerful lesson that would benefit them for the rest of their lives. Defensive routines have a limited shelf-life and cause more problems for people than they try to solve in the workplace.

This type of session is doomed from the start. If you know of anyone who conducts their performance counselling in this way, tell them they are wasting time – not saving it.

One other thing: avoid the Humpty Dumpty effect. You remember Humpty Dumpty had a great fall and all the king's horses and all the king's men couldn't put Humpty together again. The lesson for performance counselling is this. When you pull someone's defensive routines away from them you are breaking up their patterns of how they do things. So far so good. But they often feel taken apart – a bit like Humpty Dumpty. Unless you know that you are able to put them together again – don't do it. I can think of many people who are good at taking 'people apart'; but there are many more who don't know how to put people back together again. If you want to strengthen your employees and their performance at work – don't break them. If you do, it's not performance counselling you are doing. It's Humpty Dumpty.

Open mindedness versus closed mindedness

Miracles apart, don't expect employees suddenly to abandon their defensive routines. But by adopting an open-minded approach to performance counselling you can enable and empower people to see their defensive routines for what they are. When their defensive routines no longer work for them or, worse still, actively prevent them from achieving their goals you can use performance counselling to help them to change.

You need to start from where the person is *now*. Once you have built rapport and established a relationship where the person trusts you, then and only then will they consider loosening up their defensive routines and trying to change their habitual ways of managing themselves and their work. Remember it is not just the employee who is in counselling – it is the employee in relationship to you. From an open-versus-closed mindedness point of view this means the manager and the employee both need to appreciate when they are either being defended and closed-minded or accessible and open-minded during counselling. If one is open-minded and the other closed off – some progress may be made, but not of any significance. Where both are defended and closed-minded both the manager and the employee are likely to get caught up in the 'we have been here before' cycle of counselling – lots of inputs without any observable progress or changes in outputs.

The open-closed mindedness matrix

Clearly the ideal position to get to in performance counselling is where you and the person participating can be open-minded with each other. I call this double-open. When two people are in the double-open position, they are being 'up front' with each other and they can address their energies to working on tracking down and working on the real problems they face in their lives and at work. The other positions limit open communication and impede progress in improving personal problems or overcoming performance difficulties.

The worst position to get into is where you and the person in the

| | | MANAGER | |
		OPEN-MINDED	CLOSED-MINDED
E M P L O Y E E T	OPEN-MINDED	DOUBLE-OPEN	MANAGER-OPEN EMPLOYEE-CLOSED
	CLOSED-MINDED	MANAGER-OPEN EMPLOYEE-CLOSED	DOUBLE CLOSED

counselling session are closed-minded. The double-closed position. Double-closed is exemplified very well in a classic sketch in Monty Python's Flying Circus – 'The Argument Room'. The first closed-minded person asks 'Is this the argument room?' and immediately the occupant of the room rasps back 'No it isn't!' and the two men then fall into a never-ending spiral of 'Yes it is,' 'No it isn't'. In other words, they get nowhere at all because of their closed-minded approach to each other. Each has a fixed view of the world, a view that is unyielding and based on the belief that they are right and everything anybody else says is wrong.

If you conduct performance counselling like this – and there are some who do – you will get lots of heated arguments and frayed tempers. All recipes for poor performance, stress at work and low job satisfaction. Being in double-closed also prevents you achieving the fundamental goal of performance counselling: the identification of relevant issues that can be better managed by individuals in their private lives and in their organizations. If you want to accomplish this, you should vigilantly avoid the double-closed position in performance counselling.

Fear – the final frontier

It is just about here that performance counselling often fails. Why? Because fear gets in the way of real change, real progress and the breakthrough to new and valued ways of dealing with personal problems and attitudes towards work. Fear is the final frontier in performance counselling. Fear casts a long shadow. Stanley Baldwin knew this when he observed that 'everything we face cannot be changed, but nothing can be changed until we face it'.

Unless fear is faced, embraced and overcome change will not happen. Sometimes it is fear of change that prevents successful performance counselling from making any further progress; sometimes it is fear of the unknown; and sometimes it is fear of fear itself that prevents real change and the discovery and blooming of fresh ideas, initiatives and energetic performances at work.

In the *Master Manager*, R. G. H. Sui reminds us that: 'People in general, however, have always been fearful of the unknown. They have always felt much more comfortable in following the well-trodden path littered with facts from clanging bandwagons. It is also understandable why many executives, being all too human, also reflect the same fears and preferences.' We can add from our own experience – even when they know that path to be wrong, dangerous and damaging to themselves, their colleagues, and even their company. On other occasions, it will be the fear of the known that obstructs further effective performance counselling. Sometimes it will be fear of fear itself. And at yet other times it may not be the fear of change but of the consequences that follow in its wake. Whatever the fear is that prevents us from the changes we have been moving towards making, you can be sure of one thing: fear of change is real to people. It is a serious matter and if change is to come about, it has to be dealt with.

Overcoming the wall of fear

Fear is a roadblock to change. In performance counselling, you and the person in counselling have to find ways of removing those road-blocks that are mutually acceptable and at a pace that does not sabotage the trust, respect and open-mindedness you have established with each other. How many times have you got to the point of a real breakthrough with an employee when what in fact happened was a breakdown in communication between you and them? Fear, like the Berlin Wall, can be overcome and it is worth the effort. For some it may mean going into the grey and dark areas of a person's life. Significant changes often take place when people enter their own darkness with you. There is a saying in counselling that it is 'only in the darkness that you see the stars come out'. It is therefore very important that you enable employees to work through the 'black patches' in their working lives. Generating trust and openness pro-vides a candle where people can examine the kinds of changes they may want to make to themselves or their situation at work. With your help, people at work will be able to scale their own Berlin Wall. Even when things look very bleak managers would do well to recall the empowering insights of the inspiring leader Richard Byrd – 'Few men in their lifetime come anywhere near exhausting the resources dwelling within them.' The imprisoning energy that is wasted through fear can then be transposed and realized into energy for real and lasting change.

The four faces of fear

Fear has four faces: fear of what we know about ourselves; of what others know about us; of what we don't know but might discover about ourselves; and fear about what we and others don't know but might discover about each other. These four faces of fear can be seen at work. Fear can be very stressful for employees, for ourselves and for colleagues.

One of the great ways of managing fear is to face up to it – bring it out into the open. When fear is faced, people change and grow. Facing fear empowers people to become fearless. It also helps them to find out if what they fear is simply 'a phantom of their mind'.

When you use performance counselling at work, don't simply focus on the objectives or stated actions from the last session you had with a person. Make sure you work together in a climate of trust and confidence to identify and remove the fears people have about themselves – and yourself. Fear has got in the way of most things in the lives of individuals. Fear prevents action: like Lennie in John Steinbeck's novel *Of Mice and Men,* when people are frightened they 'don't want no trouble'.

FEAR KNOWN TO SELF	FEAR KNOW TO OTHERS
FEAR NOT KNOWN TO SELF	FEAR NOT KNOWN TO OTHERS

Having a sound relationship based on trust, a sense of belonging and the perception that you care about people is essential if you are to get anywhere in performance counselling. When people trust and feel trusted, when they believe they belong, when they have confidence that you care, a wonderful thing happens. They are prepared to identify their fears and explore the unknown – those areas of life and work that have been blocking change. For the first time you find people talking about what really matters to them – what fears they have about work, you, themselves and others. And, even more surprisingly, they often tell you they have a fear of change, but they don't know what it is. That's progress.

When you listen and hear people at work telling you what their fears are or wanting to find out what they fear about themselves that prevents them from being happier or having a more fulfilling life at work, why is that such good news? It's good news for three reasons. First, your counselling relationship is strong enough for them to be able to disclose to you what really matters to them. Second, they have chosen you – not you them – to empower them to come to terms with their fears. Third, and extremely important, they are ready to change and try to find new solutions to their personal and work-related problems.

Facing up to the fear of change

If you want to help someone release their own untapped resources for change get them to utilize the fear they have got. Why? Because fear is energy that is used to hold the person back from making important changes in themselves. Fear provides the fuel for new action to solve personal and performance problems at work.

So what can be done when you find people who have begun to realize that fear is holding them back from making changes in their lives? The first thing most managers often do is to urge them to 'grow up' – to not be 'a softy', stop 'being wimpish'. This is the old, worn and increasingly unproductive macho culture of 'counselling'.

What should we do then? You can begin by congratulating the individual on taking the first courageous steps towards facing up to their personal or work-based fears. Second, point out to them that their fears are a tremendous resource of energy that has been available to them and they can now learn to use in new and useful ways. Finally, make it clear that they have already started to change by the very fact that they have started to talk to you about their fears and how you can work together if they want to find out what they need to change in their personal and working lives. When you have got this far in performance counselling, you will have achieved what every enlightened manager who genuinely cares for employees wants to achieve: a good working relationship with others which allows them to be happy and resourceful at work. If you are a manager trying to empower people to become more resourceful and change, it can seem a daunting challenge. But remember this: inside the shell of fear people build around themselves lies a kernel of courage. By tapping into that courage and enabling employees to believe in themselves, you will have given them a most precious gift – the courage to change.

Assignments

Complete these assignments on your own or with other significant people in your work group/team/department/organization/private life.

- Which defence mechanisms do you typically use at work and with others outside of work?
- How are these useful to you/others?
- What are the limits of using these defence mechanisms?
- What are the desirable/undesirable consequences for you/your family/friends/work associates/colleagues?
- When you look at your department or team what are the defence mechanisms encountered and supported by them? How helpful/unhelpful is this for you/them?
- What have you done to become more open-minded in your organization this year? Which areas do you still need to work on? Why?
- Which fears prevent you from changes you want to make in your life?
- What fears do you need to explore that you are unsure about?
- What are the benefits to you to bring your fears out in to the open?
- How many specific ways are there to help people release themselves from fear and find fresh energy for themselves and their work?

4

RAISING THE ICEBERG – LESSONS FROM THE TITANIC

'As a patterning device, the brain almost certainly has no equal. It is capable of sorting and storing virtually every piece of data it takes in.' *Gordon Dryden and Dr Jeanette Vos*

Here's a question for you. If the captain of the *Titanic* knew the ship was heading for an iceberg what do you think he would have done? One option is that he could have taken emergency action to avoid the catastrophe that wrecked the ship and took so many lives. Another is he could have anticipated there would be trouble ahead and proceeded more slowly. Another is that he could have listened more carefully to the crew and navigated a different course safely round or through the field of icebergs. Why then did the terrible disaster occur? The *Titanic* story is important for us because it illustrates some essential features for those involved in practical counselling. In the first instance the captain wasn't really listening to his crew. Secondly, he didn't have the necessary information. Third, he had embarked on a course that was difficult to change – both because of his decision to carry on and the difficulty of altering course with such a huge ship. The story about the *Titanic* may or may not be true, that's not important: what it does do nicely is to illustrate three essential lessons for managers engaging in performance counselling.

Lesson one – 'I hear what you are saying'

The first lesson is that we must genuinely listen to what people say to us. Much of the time listening is not what we are doing; instead we adopt a pretence of listening to what employees or colleagues say to us. Try a little experiment. Any time today just listen for the phrase 'I hear what you are saying'. Maybe you even use it yourself! One way to find out if you really do hear what people say to you in performance counselling is to test it out for your understanding. Instead of failing to listen and vaguely saying 'I hear what you say', enquire and ask – as below:

Examples

- So am I right ... in your opinion you are feeling...?
- It's your belief that...
- Is this what you mean when you say...?
- By that do you mean that...?
- Now have I understood you correctly...?
- Are you saying that...?
- OK, let's see if I have got this right...
- I'd appreciate it if you would go over that just one more time...
- What is it you think I need to understand...?
- Let me see if I fully understand what you are saying...

By doing this you are making a genuine attempt to check that you have heard and understood what has been said by the person you are working with. Alongside this you are sending a covert message to the person in performance counselling that 'I want you to know I am listening to you'. Checking for understanding soon lets you and the other person know how much listening is going on. Checking understanding helps you to avoid crashing into the hidden icebergs. When you are listening with understanding you are in much safer waters to navigate the course of counselling.

Lesson two – accessing information

The hypnopsychotherapist and developer of integral therapy Stephen Brooks has a wonderful way of working with people. When Stephen finds people are stuck or engaged on a '*Titanic* course' to disaster he tells them that what they lack is information. Information is found in their personal library – and the library is the vast range of resources and memories that we have filed away in our minds.

Whenever you find someone is having problems in making important changes in their lives or in situations they would like to be different, send them to 'their library' – help them to discover what they have filed away and how they might access the information in those files so that they can apply it to their problem. If you want to avoid the icebergs in your life you need to know a lot about icebergs. You need to know how many there are. Where they are. You need to know how close you are to them and whether an alternative course of action will get you to your destination.

In other words, if you want to empower people to take charge of the direction in their lives, they need to have information; they need to know what it is they want to change, how long it is going to take them, just what period of time they are going to work on deciding what they are specifically intent on changing, what it is they want to achieve and how much it is going to cost them to give up their present patterns of behaviour – the ones they say they are stuck with or don't know how to overcome. All of this means being able to get inside the library of our mind, select the appropriate files and access information that is relevant to our situation.

When I was doing some team work at an international airport recently, there were lots of suggestions 'flying' around the table about how we should solve a particular problem the team faced. Proposals came thick and fast. They were ignored, judged, dispensed with in seconds. I had to point out to the team that they were in great danger of losing valuable information and they needed to 'hear' the substance of the ideas and access even more information before they lost their way in the process. So wherever you find people are heading for collision with an iceberg and need to take avoiding action, help them to see that the first thing they need is relevant information. Without information you end up guessing and just hoping everything will turn out right.

Empowering through uncovering information

Empowering people to grow and change means accessing and uncovering information. Uncovering information lets managers know what they are really 'dealing with'. Uncovering information is like raising icebergs out of the water. In performance counselling managers spend less time telling others what they should do to solve their problems than they do in uncovering the information that will be relevant to the individual for the problems they have to work on. Managers need to learn to raise icebergs in their counselling of others.

Uncovering information

Spot the difference between the two manager-employee interactions below. One is the advice-giving, the telling manager, the one who exemplifies the 'I know best' approach to counselling an employee. The other is concerned with raising the information iceberg.

Advice-giving session

James (manager). OK, Brian, come in and sit down and let's get this problem sorted out.

Brian. Thanks James (sounding grateful).

James. Now Brian, it's those delivery dates for the Northern Region. We need to improve them by 50 per cent otherwise you lose the business and we have to lay off some of the drivers.

Brian. Well, I thought we might need to consider...

James (butting in). There isn't anything to consider – it's all decided. Just put things right and get moving on this. It's your head that's on the line. Do you understand me? (sounding threatening).

Brian. Oh sure, you're not interested in what is going on – you just want results.

James. Right first time, Brian my boy. So go to it....

Brian. It's not going to work. I can tell you why.

James. I'm late for a meeting, Brian. Just make sure you sort it out.

Raising the information iceberg

James. Good morning, Brian. Glad you could make it to look at the delivery dates issue.

Brian. Yeah, James it's urgent. I am getting panicky, and we need to find a solution soon.

James. A solution for what specifically?

Brian. For the problem of delivery dates.

James. How is this a problem for you?

Brian. You know, everyone is saying we should be delivering within three days now instead of within seven days from receipt of orders.

James. Everyone? Isn't anybody happy with our delivery dates. I'm surprised we have any customers at all.

Brian. Well, no, that's not quite correct.

James. OK, how correct can you be?

Brian. Pretty close, really. I mean 89 per cent of our customers are pleased with our delivery dates at present. (Raised iceberg)

James. What makes you so sure of this?

Brian. Our customer care department completed a survey last month and came up with these figures. (Raised iceberg)

James. So is it the other 11 per cent you are wanting to work on?

Brian. Yes, I think so – in the light of this new information (Raised iceberg)

James. What do we know about this 11 per cent? (Raised iceberg)

Brian. Ah... We know they place two or three orders a year.

James. How many?

Brian. Most place two orders per year?

James. And what is particularly important about these orders?

Brian. Now you mention it I suppose I realize for the first time they all come from Billy Green's sales sector over on the islands. (Raised iceberg)

James. So let me see if we understand each other. You are saying the vast majority of our customers are satisfied with our delivery dates but a small percentage from the islands in Billy Green's territory would like to have their delivery dates improved upon.

Brian. Yeah, that's what I'm saying.

James. Brian, what seems to be the next best step to take to resolve this issue?

Brian. Eh... from what we have been saying it might make sense to speak to Billy Green and maybe the drivers to look at ways this specific sector for our products and services can improve on delivery dates.

Three weeks later

James. Congratulations on sorting out the delivery dates for the islands.

Brian. It was surprisingly easy after that last meeting with you, James.

James.What surprised you exactly?

Brian. Oh... the fact that I didn't need to talk to the drivers.

James. You didn't need to talk to the drivers – Who *did* you talk to?

Brian. I spoke with Billy Green. I took a leaf out of your book and tried to discover information that he had that might be useful for him, his customers and the reputation of the delivery team here at the plant.

James. And what did you discover, Brian?

Brian. I found that Billy takes the orders from his customers in plenty of time – on Thursday mornings to be precise – but he didn't send them to us until the Monday morning. That was a gap of four days before posting them and five or sometimes six days before they reached the plant.

James. You say he didn't post them on the same day and there was a gap of four days before posting them to us. How are things different now?

Brian. Now Billy sends his orders in on the Thursdays and the plant processes them and gets the orders delivered to the customer on time.

James. What have you learned from all of this, Brian?

Brian. I've definitely learned how important it is to discover the kind of information that is needed to deal with these kinds of problems. Another thing, James. I learned how finding the right information means you can tackle the real problem.

James. What was the real problem for you?

Brian. I thought I was dealing with a delivery problem, when all the time it was really sorting out with Billy Green how he returned his orders promptly to the plant.

James. Brian, I'd like to congratulate you on finding that information and preventing a worthless and costly major enquiry into how the plant operates, and avoiding the disruption schedules of the drivers, and possibly unnecessary conflict between ourselves and our island customers.

Brian. Thanks, James. I really mean it – thanks a lot.

James. By the way, what happened to that panicky feeling you had – have you got it now?

Brian. What panicky feeling?

James. OK, Brian, well done. I guess we don't have any more problems with delivery dates now.

Lesson three – changing course

However, sometimes even having significant information will not be enough for someone to solve their personal or work-related problems. The employee who is worried about the 30 per cent rise in accidents on his shift can stop worrying when new safety regulations put into practice reduce this figure by half, or the female supervisor who is anxious over how well she is doing in building a production team when she gets a very satisfactory appraisal from her boss and encouraging feedback from her nascent team. But there are many times when information itself will be quite insufficient to make changes. Take for example people with performance problems through the personal abuse of alcohol. They can know where they drink too much; they can pinpoint what sort of people they mix with and under what specific circumstances they become drunk. Now try asking them to give up drinking too much alcohol. The result: they carry on drinking.

Examples like this show us how it is often very difficult for people with problems to change their behaviour. They find that despite having information about their behaviour, they cannot change course. Like Jack Lemmon in the film 'Days of Wine and Roses' they can't find a way of giving up – easily. Changing course means helping people to face up to the enormity of the changes they see they have to make. Giving up drinking alcohol or cutting down may seem easy for most people, but not for the person who has established a pattern of behaviour where alcohol is part of the chain of command. Some individuals are anchored to alcohol but it is not just alcohol: it can be anything – sex, overeating, gambling, drugs and other forms of personal abuse.

Personal habits – the links in the chain

Changing course means being able to break the links in the chain that anchor you to the things you want to change – the things you need to get rid of in your life but don't yet know how to.

When people are anchored like this they need professional help. An on-site or off-site confidential employee counselling service can provide this source of help. It backs up managers and occupational healthcare centres in the work they do with employees. A personal stress counselling service helps people to identify those things they want to change in their personal or working lives. It helps people at work personally to realize the adage that 'not everything I face can be changed, yet nothing can be changed until I face it.' Facing up to what needs to be changed is a big step forward in performance counselling. It means people no longer deny their problems at work. They no longer pretend everything is all right. When you find someone who is stuck with a problem they want to get rid of, it is they who must first tell you that they are ready to do something about it.

Secondary gain

One of the reasons people find difficulty in giving up habits they find unacceptable is secondary gain. Secondary gain means just what it suggests: there is nothing worth changing for because the person gets something out of not changing. The secretary who stands abuse from the boss does not change it. Why? Because it is the only time she gets attention in the office. People who drink too much carry on because they gain 'friends' through the fog of alcohol. The people who spread rumours and gossip at work find they want to give it up but can't because of the sense of power or recognition it gives them.

People find thousands of ways of achieving secondary gain. Unfortunately, it is often at the expense of being unable to change course. Changing course is often blocked by secondary gains. It's like you are watching a movie where the Phantom of the Opera appears: you are desperate to avoid a confrontation but at the same time fascinated by the possibility of seeing him face to face. When people want to grow and change but are stuck like this, they are saying: 'I have a pattern I want to change but I can't.' Performance counselling enables them to break the pattern. This is the start of further progress and real change.

Breaking the pattern – forming the foundations for change

Some changes we can make automatically; others take more time. If you decide you don't want to watch the sports channel on TV you select another programme by simply pressing a button on the channel selector. You 'change your mind'. In the supermarket you don't want your usual brand of cereal and you try another. These changes take only mini-moments and they are done.

Breaking habits of a lifetime or sometimes thoughts, feelings and behaviours that bring us secondary gains, seems more difficult. Overcoming shyness, managing jealousy, increasing confidence, controlling drinking, stopping lying, starting to get rid of some people in our lives and bring others into it, setting realistic objectives instead of unreachable and fantastic ones – these are only some of the patterns people say they want to change but can't. Is there a secret for changing when you want to change and can't? And if there is one, what is it?

The Taylor secret for success

I'm reminded of a story about a schoolteacher who was extremely successful with pupils who had failed in all the other classes in the school. After this pattern of failure they often ended up getting the best results. They were no more dull, dim, impetuous or gifted than the other pupils in the school and everybody wondered why hers did so well. The teacher – let's call her Miss Taylor – was eagerly talked about by her colleagues, each speculating on 'the secret of her success'. Some thought it was a particular teaching method that Miss Taylor alone had developed. Others believed Miss Taylor benefited more from having been to university. There was even a theory that the room Miss Taylor taught in was influenced by the benevolent and heavenly spirit of the founding headmaster and this enlightened the children. The speculation and rumours about her success were plentiful and multiplied by the day. But all were wrong.

One day, in the staffroom, it dawned on the other teachers to *ask* Miss Taylor how she could so consistently help her pupils break their failed patterns of learning and make the changes that brought them success. Do you know what happened next? It was a revelation. Miss Taylor never expounded on any great theories of education; she never detailed the depths of her 'secret teaching methods' or the Taylor techniques of teaching; and she never claimed to be guided by the spirit of the founding headmaster. What she did say was quite simple. 'I help the children discover their belief that there is no such thing as *can't*.' 'And how do you do that,' they asked. Her reply: 'By encouraging them to explore important questions and express themselves the way you are doing now.' The teachers suddenly realized how caring but critical questions can break unwanted patterns and lead to the creation of changes in their lives. They also discovered for themselves how Miss Taylor developed a collaborative partnership with her pupils in their pursuit of personal change.

Cultivating a collaborative relationship

Encouraging expression – the beginnings of unblocking

Miss Taylor's secrets of success are very pertinent for counselling those people who say they want to change but can't. Encouraging expression and pursuing caring but critical questions starts to remove the blocks that prevent change. These very first small but significant steps facilitate the process of change. Managers who really care for their colleagues and other employees can empower them to get rid of the roadblocks that are holding them up from personal growth and making significant changes in the patterns of their working or personal lives. But unblocking means taking risks.

Risking caring

The manager must risk caring for all employees as individuals in their own right. When people recognize you care for them they take risks. People need to feel safe enough with you to take risks; without risk-taking of this kind there can be no unblocking and therefore no real change.

If performance counselling is about anything it is about caring, and caring does not come easily. It is easier to resort to narrow thinking. Pronouncing policies and procedures, 'laying down the law', 'going by the book' and 'throwing the book' at employees are proven recipes for narrow and rigid thinking. It prevents change. People at the receiving end of this kind of managing don't take risks, don't feel cared for and quite rightly are not prepared to change.

Raising the Iceberg

The project team manager

Here is how a good performance counselling session can go when you care for people and encourage them to express themselves. Notice how the careful use of questions helps to start unblocking their abilities, motivation and self-esteem.

Philip. Chris, I'm glad we have managed to find this time to meet... I realize you are busy like me... So where would you like to begin?

Chris. Well, it is something that's bothered me for a long time now. But I can't seem to do anything about it.

Philip. Mmm... something you are really concerned about?

Chris. Yeah... It's been on my mind since I became Project Manager.

Philip. Would that be something you want to talk about a bit more...?

Chris. I would, but I don't see a way out of my problem.

Philip. It seems you're at a dead end....

Chris. I know. I feel so angry.

Philip. About...?

Chris. I promised Jenny a place on the Project team months ago and now I find the budget doesn't allow for an extra person on the team.

Philip. Let me see if I understand you Chris. You feel trapped and angry at the moment, and it has something to do with promising Jenny a place on the Project team which you now think you are not in a position to do.

Chris. Right. Yes that's made it a bit clearer. I do see it that way. You know, I think you are the only person who understands me.

Philip. Sometimes it helps you to untangle tangled problems. Tangled problems are a bit like knitting, you know – once you understand the pattern you can decide where you are going next.

Chris. Yes, I suppose I do want to untangle this now I know what's involved.

Philip. You know what is involved. . . .

Chris. It's my feelings of letting down Jenny. She'll think that I'm a real swine.

Philip. Chris, how do you know that?

Chris. Well because... oh, I don't know for sure. I imagine she would.

Philip. I'm wondering if you know of any other time when Jenny was promised something and it didn't work out.

Chris. Oh, yes. Don't you remember the Intertech contract?

Philip. Sure. Hmmmm... What happened?

Chris. They cancelled at the last minute and Jenny missed out on that one.

Philip. Can you remember how she took it?

Chris. Yes. She said she was disappointed but that was the nature of this kind of work.

Philip. Can you see any connection between this time and that contract that might tell you how to deal with Jenny?

Chris. Now you mention it, I can. I can tell her how personally concerned I am that she is not on this Project team.

Philip. But...?

Chris. But that like other project contracts we have had to cut down on the size of the team.

Philip. When would be the best time for you to go ahead and do this Chris?

Chris. Sometime that suits Jenny and me to meet in private.

Philip. Well done, Chris. You've started to untangle the knitting. I'd be interested to find out how you can benefit from your meeting with Jenny.

Chris. Sure, I'll keep you posted. Oh, and thanks.

Philip. Good to see you again, Chris. Keep in touch.

Congratulating

One of the most effective ways of unblocking and releasing energy for change in performance counselling is to congratulate the person on their achievements to date. Did you notice how Philip congratulated Chris on those occasions and he became less blocked and started to change? When was the last time you can remember congratulating an individual for wrestling with a personal or work-related problem? Or did you simply hand out 'good advice' about how they *should* manage their problem. Unfortunately there are far too many 'should' managers in organizations. Just recall last week for a moment:

- How many 'shoulds' in how many situations do you recall?
- What kinds of situations were they?
- Who was involved?
- What was the outcome for (1) you and (2) the others involved?

Now build up a 'should' picture in your mind or draw or write it down on paper. There will probably be quite a number of 'should nots' in there as well. When you have done that, do the same for the occasions when you have found yourself congratulating people at work. Tally up the shoulds, should nots and do the same for congratulating others. How well did you do? If your shoulds and should nots outweigh congratulating others you need to change.

Congratulating others does a wonderful thing. It says to them 'you are important', 'you matter', 'you count', 'I believe in you.'

Charles Schweb, a multi-millionaire steel executive, when asked for his great secret of helping people grow, unblock themselves, solve personal problems and contribute to the staggering success of his company, said: 'I consider my ability to arouse enthusiasm among the men the greatest asset I possess, and the way to develop the best that is in a man is by appreciation and encouragement. There is nothing else that so kills the ambitions of a man as criticism. I never criticize anyone. I am hearty in my approbation and lavish in my praise.'

If you want to get people unstuck and moving in a different direction start congratulating them more often.

The collaborative relationship – a platform for action

A collaborative relationship in performance counselling provides you with a platform for action. If there is no collaborative relationship people often end up creating more problems than you started out to solve. Performance counselling is a two-way process. I listen to you; you listen to me. I care about you; you care about me. I question you; you question me. If you want people not only to solve their problems but release new possibilities in themselves, then consciously cultivate a collaborative relationship with them.

Collaboration is about caring and questioning. Just telling people what to do does not work in performance counselling. It discourages them from taking risks. It prevents them exploring problems, possibilities and taking action. Advice-giving is the kiss of death for people who need to change for themselves, their colleagues and their company. The only dubious attraction about receiving advice, as the writer Scott Fitzgerald knew, is 'you don't have to take it'.

I recently asked a great manager to define the difference between traditional managing and managing through performance counselling. This is what he had to say: 'Traditional managing is where I advise and lead or channel people into a dimly lit tunnel and say it's OK if you do this and this and this and then I lead them out into the light at the end of the tunnel – managing through performance counselling is where we say to each other, let's first find the tunnel, then, OK here is the tunnel, let's go in together – and during our journey through the tunnel we both learn new things and find we need each other to get out to the light at the other end. But they lead me out... I follow them at the other end – that's the difference. And a very important difference it is too.'

If you spot yourself giving advice, *stop,* and ask yourself this question: how much is this helping me and how much is it empowering the person I am counselling? If you are honest with yourself, the chances are your advice will be sound for you but not for them. And even though the person in counselling decides on the same course of action as you would have advised that is still not a good reason for giving advice. Why? Because in discovering what the issues are that face them people becomes motivated to solve 'their' problem. The problem belongs to them – and so do any attempted solutions. When you can share in the process towards helping a person realize this position, you can feel confident you have formed a truly collaborative relationship.

Assignments

- How much of an advice-giver are you? How do you know?
- Give some examples of where you have been an advice-giver. What were the benefits/drawbacks?
- When have you empowered other people to take risks in changing themselves or their situation? How did you do it? What were the results for them/you/your organization?
- Where can you best use the building of further collaborative relationships with others in your organization?
- How many times in the last few days at work have you congratulated someone on what they have done/what they have tried to do/are trying to do/for wrestling with a difficult problem? And did you really mean it?
- What secondary gains are people in your organization/ department/office/depot/plant/getting from problems they have but are not changing?
- How have you facilitated or frustrated them in facing up to changes they need to make in their lives?
- Give some examples of how you have empowered people through careful listening, accessing relevant information and changing course on a problem or issue that is important to them.
- Get together with your colleagues or work team. Examine, share, compare and listen to each other about how you can further develop accessing of appropriate information and taking collaborative action with people in your organization.

5

BEYOND ROLE PERFORMANCE

'We do know that everyone's potential goes far beyond anything ever realized.' *Peter Klinz*

Work and roles

Work and roles are like actors in movies. An organization that casts
its players into clear roles with snappy scripts and a great director
knows what it is about. Players know what performances are expected
of them in the unfolding drama of their organizational life. They learn
their positions and their lines.

These role players become more necessary the bigger the organization. A giant like Chrysler needed Lee Iacocca to shake up the roles
people were playing and to make the Chrysler corporation 'a number
one player on the world stage'. But Iacocca did much more than that.
He realized how to get the best out of people. He was tough. He axed
jobs. He was demanding. He led by making difficult decisions. But he
did something else. He inspired people to go beyond their roles. He
reached the whole person. People at Chrysler gave more than what
was expected. They were more than simple role occupants riding out
the act of making Chrysler successful.

Iacocca was not a bully but a person who had found in himself
new resources to shape up the troops at Chrysler. Authority and fear
had motivated Chrysler employees. Even though there are disagree-
ments about whether Iacocca was a leader or a louse, he was a

phenomenon – the first hero manager. At the same time, he made many enemies. And when he wasn't 'minding the store' there was always the threat that people would slacken off their great efforts to compete with Ford and oppose the Japanese invasion of vehicle markets in the USA.

Organizational Oscars

One of the fundamental attractions of playing roles in organizations is the potential and promise of putting in a powerful performance – one that gives the players the equivalent of an organizational Oscar. Oscars come in many forms: promotions, selecting your own office, choosing on which floor of a new building to have the office. These are all Oscars for outstanding role performances in organizations.

The problem is that not everybody can be the star. This is where roles in the theatre of work have become limiting. On top of this the world has changed. It's changed so fast. Future shock is here already. Static roles were fine when the organization had a stable and predictable environment in which to conduct its business. That has gone. Instead there is rapid change at a pace which is not going to stop to make room for the fixed roles people want to play or the way organizations structure themselves.

People not roles are at the centre of the thriving organization. What organizations require from people is role flexibility. As Tom Peters observes, we still need to thrive as people and as organizations. The problem is how to help people to grow and to enjoy thriving on chaos. The real world of people and organizations is a daily struggle to make sense of chaos and cash in on it. Managers, however, can help people to overcome their role limitations and role difficulties.

The first thing to be done is to give people the opportunity to sort out their role difficulties with you. When roles are no longer appropriate – when people are in conflict with what they know is the right thing to do and how the organization says they should behave – there are problems: personal problems; problems that lead to troubled employees and troubled organizations; personal problems that arise from work and undermine health, well-being and job performance; problems that arise outside of work which people bring into work to affect their effectiveness in the work they are trying to do. Chaos in work and chaos outside combine and put enormous obstacles in the way of people and the roles they perform. Role-based organization can no longer solve these problems of personal performance at work. If we want people thriving in today's work environments we need to get beyond the roles we expect people to perform. We need to reach the whole person. Roles only have any real significance if you release the personal energies, innovation and commitment of the people who occupy them.

Reaching the whole person

Building a collaborative relationship empowers managers to reach the whole person. So what does reaching the whole person actually mean? It means managers being able to apprehend the person and the problems they are attempting to solve at work. Having gone to the bother of being able to communicate non-defensively, you sell yourself short if you then revert to relying on the role behaviours you require from people. Managers manage people, not roles. If you are to enable people to grow and make the most of themselves at work you need to avoid becoming role-bound. When you can do this, you will have been able to remove the mask of managing and empowered the people you manage to do the same.

The Chinese have a potent proverb that captures the essence of reaching the whole person: 'You must give the bird room to fly.' Caged birds don't fly very far. Caged for a long time they forget how to fly altogether. Managers need to be able to let the people they are managing out of their cages and give them flying lessons. When they can find they can fly they will prove to you how they can perform far beyond the limitations their work-based roles have imposed upon them.

Role advantages and limitations

You can approach this question productively by asking people to outline the advantages of their roles at work. Ask them to help you understand specifically how their roles contribute to what they are trying to achieve. You can follow this up by inviting them to test out with you the value to them of carrying on with their roles without changing anything. This can be done by saying you wonder what work would be like for them if they did not have to work in the way they are at present. How would things be different? Better or worse? How much better? How much worse? As a manager you can benefit from considering alternative ways in which roles might be changed or how the person in performance counselling might do things differently – and what are the likely consequences for them, yourself and other parts of your organization. There are at least two positive outcomes of all this inviting, asking and considering: first, you will open up new possibilities for people to grow in confidence and self-worth; second, you will get a view of how people see their role difficulties and limitations as well as the way that their present roles help or hinder their contribution to the management of the organization.

Peter Gray brings this to our attention in *Action Learning and Organizational Change*. 'Frequently individuals realize that they need to clarify their own thinking about their role and then discover that a number of key people in the organization have different, sometimes conflicting ideas about their role. The difficulty may arise in that a key manager may feel that the individual has no business to intervene in a particular area, or that he is under no obligation to provide information and assistance. Thus the need to gain acceptance of a new and fuller role often becomes vital if progress is to be made. This involves the individual in identifying the limits of his role, clarifying people's expectations of his role, and negotiating a bigger role.'

The person behind the mask

The 'bigger role' is one that encompasses the whole person. Roles have proved to be very useful and contribute to productive work in a healthy workforce. But roles are like masks. They hide the real person and the resources they have to solve their own problems and those they face at work. To grow people so they get more for themselves and more for their organization we need to see the person behind the mask. Unless you can reach the person behind the role you never know them or the extra qualities they have and the special personal competencies they can bring to their work. A good analogy is the difference between American and Chinese baseball. In American baseball each player has a predefined position and a number of predictable actions they can take once the ball leaves the pitcher's hand. But in Chinese baseball the only similarity is in pitching the ball; after that players can move in any direction they think is appropriate. The difference is one has roles and role boundaries; the other has a basic principle. You occupy your role in many different ways using *all* the skills you have to solve the problem and reach your goals.

Managers need to be able to appreciate the powerful personal resources lurking in the people they work with. More than that, managers have responsibility to create a climate of caring wherein people can learn that they have permission to explore and use these new-found resources for themselves at work.

Mining the treasure within

One top manager in banking who seemed to get more from the people he worked with summed up how he did it by telling his colleagues this story. 'Getting the best from people and helping them to get the best from themselves is like working in a mine. To begin with you have to decide where to stake your claim. You then work the mine with a total commitment. You believe that one day – maybe it will be today or maybe tomorrow or in the days ahead – you will find some gems or precious metals. The fascinating thing is you aren't exactly certain when you are going to find the "treasure" within – so you have to work at finding it and help them to discover it as well. Sometimes it takes a lot of sweat. Sometimes it comes easy; and at other times you may wonder why you are putting so much effort into unearthing this treasure you believe is there. You may even wonder just occasionally whether it is worth it or not and those you are working with might feel the same. But don't give up. For there comes a time, that special moment – and there can be many of them – when you and they realize you have discovered that treasure. For some it will be gold, for others diamonds and for others rubies or some other precious find. But make no mistake, when you mine the treasure within, it will pay off for you and for them for a very long time to come. It more than compensates for the effort you may have put in.'

What a wonderful story. It has such a powerful message for all managers and anyone concerned about making the most of human resources at work. Behind every role is a person – a person who has a rich reservoir of personal resources. And you can liberate these resources by making it possible for people to become more than their roles and the limitations their roles at work place on them. This story tells us much; much more about making the most of people and empowering them to make the most of themselves at work than most textbooks on the subject.

See if you can make your own list. Just break off from what you are doing now and quickly write down all of the lessons you have learned from this story. What does it tell you about: how you work with people? how you can empower then to go beyond their role limitations? where you can begin to make it possible for others to improve their counselling of others? Do this in a work group, with your team or with someone you are concerned about right now. When you have done it make a note of your personal learnings and decide what you are going to keep the same and what you are going to change when you are counselling others about their performance at work.

Talking heads – what the brain tells us about performance counselling

Let me ask you this: if you were a miner would you use a toothpick or an ore-boring machine to get out gold from a mine? Like most managers you would probably say the boring machine; you get nowhere with a toothpick. But there is a curious thing when managers are counselling others: they seem to use the toothpick approach to talking with others. Just like being in the mine – they get nowhere. Why is this? Why is it that when two heads are supposed to be talking to each other they can't seem to communicate in a way that they understand each other? In this kind of counselling managers are 'knocking their heads against a brick wall'. Reseach in psychology has shown how to overcome these problems of communication. We can make much better use of counselling when we know what the brain tells us about counselling others.

Not one brain but two

One of the most important findings of psychologists in recent years was the discovery that the brain is divided into two hemispheres – the left and the right. Each hemisphere functions in a different way from the other. For instance, language, logic and analysis are essentially functions of the left hemisphere. Compare this with imagery, creativity and synthesis which are functions of the right brain.

Both sides of the brain are connected together by a band of nerves called the corpus callosum – a kind of transmitter system that makes it possible for the left and right sides of the brain to communicate with each other and with other people. The neuropsychology is complex but it has very significant implications for performance counselling at work.

Functions of the left hemisphere and right hemisphere

The left and right hemispheres have different functions. Between them they are responsible for logic, recognition, reason, rhythm, mathematics, visual/imagery, reading, creativity, writing, dreams, language, symbols, analysis and synthesis. Can you identify any of them? When we are communicating well with others in counselling we are able to share their reality. Working with the two sides of the

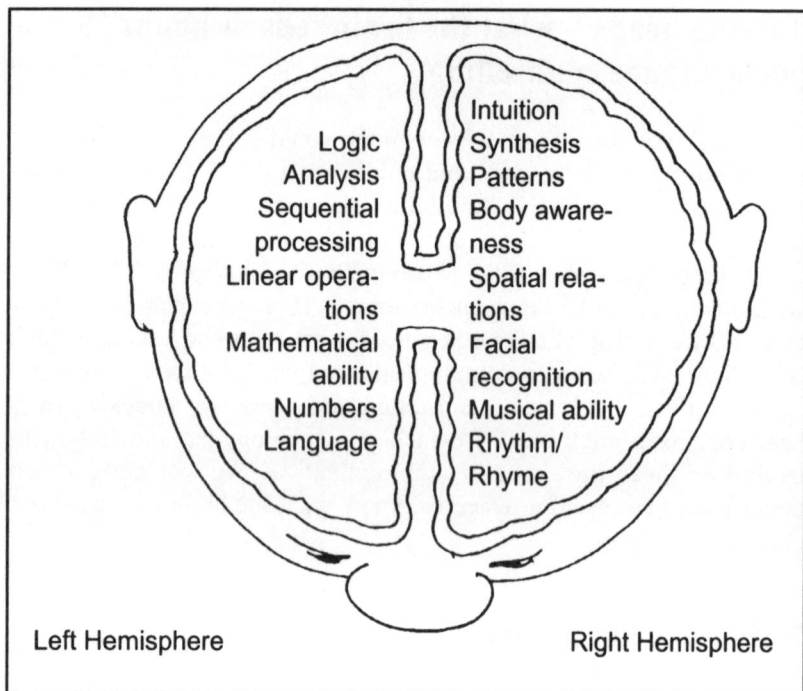

Left Hemisphere	Right Hemisphere
Logic	Intuition
Analysis	Synthesis
Sequential	Patterns
processing	Body aware-
Linear opera-	ness
tions	Spatial rela-
Mathematical	tions
ability	Facial
Numbers	recognition
Language	Musical ability
	Rhythm/
	Rhyme

brain this means when I am talking to you in analytical terms, when I am using logic in my language and emphasizing reason or calculations of numbers or written work and you are doing the same, we communicate well. When one of us is not, we have a problem.

It is the same with the right side of the brain. Suppose we were examining how best to assist a person overcome their fear of making presentations. If we ask them to feel the rhythm and regulation of their speech, see themselves before a group, spontaneously being innovative and making key points graphically, they would appreciate this counselling given that they too processed the problem either through their right brain directly or by accessing from the left to the right so they could improve their presentations.

So far so good. But what often happens when we are trying to empower people to help themselves, to do better, to unlock those personal resources we know are there within them? What often happens is that we don't know how to unlock such personal resources. Or we unwittingly but actively make it difficult for them to become more effective at running their own life. How many managers do you know who have told you, 'The harder I try with X the worse it gets', or another frequent comment, 'We have worked and worked at this but were just getting nowhere with X'. These managers are telling us something many of us secretly knew: we are unable to find the key that unlocks the personal resources of people to deal with and manage their own problems. True – at least up until now.

We now know more about the brain and how it functions. We can use what we know to enhance communication between ourselves and others and what goes on in counselling. So how specifically can we use this knowledge of the two hemispheres – the two brains and the corpus callosum – to improve counselling others and our communications with them at work?

Crossed communications

The answer lies in being able to apply an essential rule of counselling – namely, know when you are in a crossed communication. There are a number of clues you can look for here. When managers find they are unsuccessful in counselling others crossed communication is the first thing to look for.

It occurs when one person is utilizing the functions of the left brain

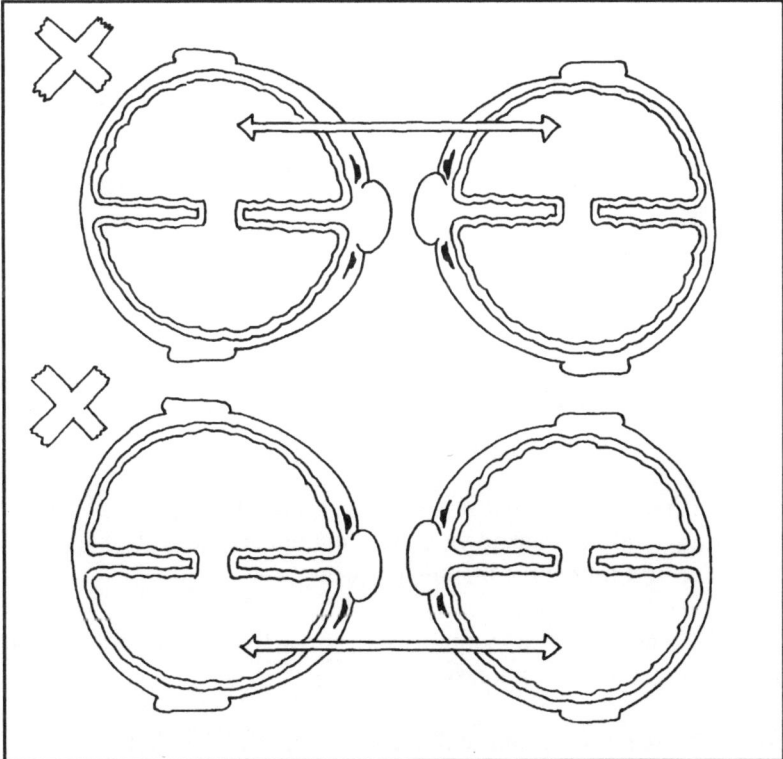

and the other is utilizing the functions of the right as they are talking to each other. The result? They don't understand each other. They have 'a communication problem'. Imagine this scene:

Crossed counselling session

Jeremy (manager). Glad you could make it this morning, Mike. Now what seems to be the specific problem today?

Mike. I, well... I can't exactly put it into words.

Jeremy. Well, you called the meeting, Mike. You should know what you're talking about.

Mike. Yeah, yeah, I do know what the problem is but I just can't say what I mean.

Jeremy. (losing patience) Try me.

Mike. Well, it's like a big door is blocking me off, and I...

Jeremy (irritated now and showing it). Look Mike I didn't come here especially this morning to talk about doors.

Mike (now his turn to be irritated). I don't understand what you're getting at.

Jeremy (now trying to show great restraint). And I still don't know why you called this meeting...

Mike (now annoyed and giving up). OK, it's always the same. You don't understand me and I don't see what you mean – most of the time you leave me out of the picture.

Jeremy. Right, right, that's it – no analysis, no breakdown of what's happening – only a breakdown in our communication – once again. If only you could follow the line of argument.

Mike. Let's not focus on that old scene now... It reminds me too much of old videos I have no interest in watching.

Jeremy (looking worn out and exasperated). Yeah, let's get back to work.

Mike. I see clearly now you don't want to help me... You just want to hang a black cloud over my ideas.

Jeremy (groans and gets up out of his seat the same time as Mike argues and leaves the room). What a way to start the week.

Why did it not work out? How did they manage to communicate the way they did? The counselling session was abandoned. Why? Because the communications were crossed. Jeremy was utilizing his left hemisphere and Mike his right. Mike talked about not being able to put it into words, pictures, seeing the problem, watching it and not wanting to focus on old scenes, and being 'left' out of the picture. Jeremy was much more left-brained. He talked of specific problems, calling a meeting, breaking down and analysing, and not following the line of argument. Are you surprised they had to abandon their counselling session?

Do two things now, right now. First write down similar crossed communications you know about. Second, say how you could have improved them. Do this before you do anything else. Now read on.

Uncrossing communications

In performance counselling you get much further by uncrossing communications, and when you can identify crossed communications it is only a short step to uncrossing them. Too many managers seem to give up when they are faced with crossed communications in counselling. You have probably guessed that the most obvious thing for Jeremy and Mike to have done was for at least one of them – or both – to utilize their communication skills to uncross their communications with each other. Let's give them another chance and see how it works out this time round.

Jeremy. Glad you could make it this morning Mike. Now what seems to be the specific problem today?

Mike. I well... I can't really put it into words.

Jeremy. How could you put it so it makes sense to you?

Mike. I've got a picture in my mind... In fact, I have worried and sweated over it so much I can see it just like a film.

Jeremy. Does that make it clearer for you Mike?

Mike. Yes, it is like a series of scenes that unfold here in the office and at the regional distribution meetings.

Jeremy. That's good. So paint these scenes for me. Make sure you are satisfied with the focus you put on them and tell me what you see happening.

Mike. I see a door – the door of your office, and when I want to come and talk it's never open for me... and... then I see myself looking all frustrated and angry because... the next picture I get is talking at the distribution meetings in the regions and not having the kind of information that lets me support your policies. I suppose because... I am not clear about your views right now.

Jeremy. Mike, maybe you could just see right now in your mind what views you would like to be clear about.

Mike. Oh, that's easy. At the moment it is the Health and Safety Policy for the regions I would need to focus on.

Jeremy. OK good Mike... Now I'd appreciate it if you could show me what that looks like on paper – maybe a flow model or diagram would help me understand how you see things unfolding.

Mike (moves towards a flipchart and starts drawing and talking at same time.) Sure. Here is how I see the problem and how we might get over it.

What happened! This time round Jeremy and Mike had a valuable counselling session. Instead of finding they were at logger heads they made genuine progress and managed to work on the real problem that was bothering Mike. But did you notice how Jeremy managed to do it? He used the feedback from Mike to align it with his right brain and conduct their counselling session with the language Mike's brain was using – the 'language' of the right brain. Jeremy adapted his replies to it. In other words, he aligned his communication to Mike so they both could make sense of each other.

Aligning communications

Aligning our communications with others makes for productive and effective counselling. After demonstrating the importance of aligning communications with employees at a recent workshop on employee empowerment, one manager came to me with a wonderful definition on the meaning of aligning communications. He said: 'Alignment in counselling is where – with a knowledge of how our brains function – I can make it possible for my brain to talk to your brain.' Absolutely right; a perfect description of alignment. Aligning communications in counselling liberates the resources of both sides of the brain. The manager who is aware of this and uses it will be able to facilitate changes in people as if by magic. You will find people asking you: How did you do that, or how did you manage to get through to him or her when nobody else could? A working practical knowledge of alignment empowers managers to communicate well with everyone in the workforce.

Left-left alignment

Logic, analysis and reason with an emphasis on reading and written communications are typical of left-left alignment in counselling or communicating with others.

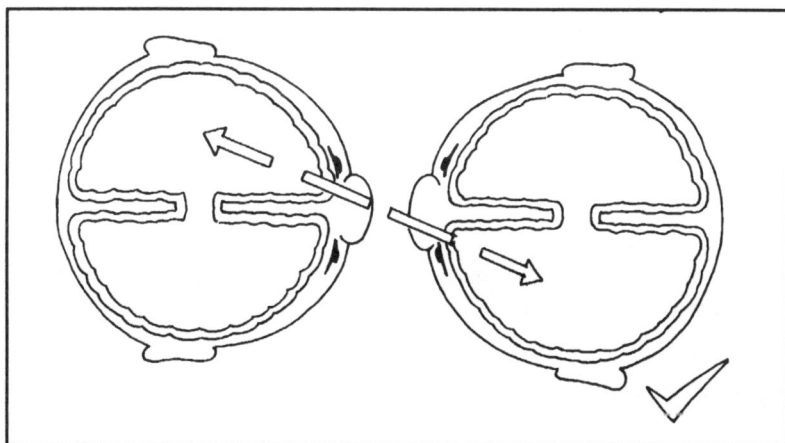

Example

Manager. I would like a full report of the main critical points you found in the accident survey.

Employee. No problem. I intend to approach my analysis by examining the frequency of specific accidents in each region designated by a postal code.

Right-right alignment

In right-right alignment, counselling is accelerated when people communicate through visual imagery, symbolic language, their emotions and creative ideas.

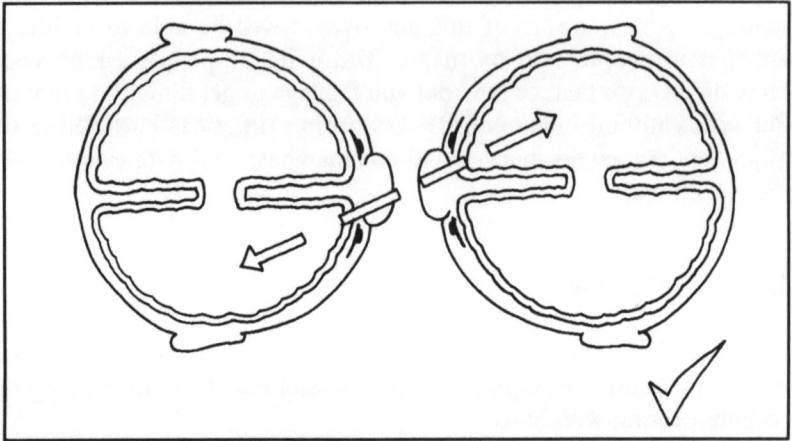

Designer. Could you understand this better if I constructed a model of the building development and designs I have in mind? It would be like showing you what a sturdy tree looked like standing high in the forest – sensational.

Customer. Sure, provided you develop the three-dimensional aspect and support your views with realistic drawings that are in harmony with the existing site. But I would get real mad if what you are creating turns out to be a poisonous pine instead of a giant oak that all the other trees could look up to.

Realignments

Left-to-right and right-to-left realignments occur where the manager is able to recognize a potentially crossed communication in counselling, and uncrosses it before it becomes a problem. The manager in fact realigns the communication with the person. In counselling, the manager utilizes the communication from an individual and aligns his communications with it.

Example – Head of employee relations in private meeting with team colleague

Peter. Phil, what analyses of the present strategy or units of it can be prepared in a report and conclusions reached for our discussions next week?

Phil. Peter, I'm not focusing on that.

Peter. OK, what are you focusing on?

Phil. All I know is that every time I see the view we take on this job I get a blinding message imprinted on my mind – it flashes on and off like a warning sign.

Peter. What does the sign say?

Phil. It's a bright heading... it flashes now just as I am talking about it.

Peter. Yes, go on. .

Phil. It says... STRESS COST THIS COMPANY £500,000 THIS YEAR.

Peter. Is that it? What else is there... what else do you see?

Phil. Looking at the rest of it... there are lots of figures I remember from the incidence of the stress survey and the causes of stress at work. There are also a host of reasons and costs attached to them. Yes, they are all popping up just like you would see them on a computer screen.

Peter. How about it if I make notes for the discussion from what you see and you...

Phil. I will map out... the main... points I want to develop... and take our perspective from them.

Peter. That's really looking good, Phil. . . and I can now put my arguments around those areas and make a forceful case for doing something about stress and its costs to the company.

The corpus callosum – your friendly traffic cop

Have you noticed what has been happening in these talking heads sessions? Why is it people have no problems in communicating in their meetings with each other? They have to be in alignment or have their communications appropriately realigned so they can make sense of each other and the worlds which they inhabit at work. This is very important. However, the alignment and realignment comes about because the bit in between the two brains – the corpus callosum – the 'traffic cop' – makes sure the traffic of communication is travelling back and forth through routes that the drivers understand. The traffic cop helps to relay communications and sends signals back and forth to the two hemispheres of the brain. The traffic cop allows communications to shuttle back and forth between the logical analytical language brain, and the symbolic, patterning, holistic intuitive brain.

Problems in communication and counselling arise when our two brains are not speaking to each other. When you have problems in communicating with colleagues or in counselling sessions with people, check out your 'traffic cop'. If you fail to understand each other, are getting nowhere or don't see eye-to-eye, or don't hear the message someone is trying to get over to you, or you want to get people to feel the importance of what you are saying, there is a problem with alignment in your communications with them.

Check out with the traffic cop if you need to take a different route to get to your destination. It's the traffic cop that is the commander of your communication channels. It's the traffic cop that tells you whether you are on the motorway or heading up a one-way street in the wrong direction. So if you want to make the most of talking with others in meetings or in private counselling sessions, get your traffic cop to give you the information which will be appropriate for your work with them. Get to know your traffic cop and you will be able to access all the roads that allow you to make the most of 'talking heads'.

Counselling – the collaborative mission

Counselling works when you work with the person in counselling. Simply telling them what to do won't work. Collaboration is the name of the game. You can understand collaboration in counselling in different ways; it's in many textbooks on counselling.

One way of experiencing what that collaboration is like more directly is to look out of your window or go for a walk. The moment you move your body it is collaborating with you. It gets up, takes you to the window or out into the street. It moves your legs and keeps you standing up straight or allows you to bend or move your eyes. It collaborates with you in doing these things and many more because you have worked out how to collaborate with it. You don't just sit there and say, 'OK come on body get moving, we're going out.' If you do it just stays sat there – not moving or doing what you commanded it to do. So what's the difference? Collaboration. Through collaboration you and your body have found out how to do these very complex things and make them seem easy.

It's the same secret in counselling. In counselling, you can discover how to do very complex things and yet in time it seems easy. It becomes like a dance where the person in counselling and you both find how you can not 'tread on each other's toes'. By learning the steps you can make in order to achieve new and agreed behaviour, new thinking and new ways of feeling about work and each other you make counselling a shared mission.

Ready for Everest – explorers in the Antarctic and anyone for a safari?

Sir Edmund Hillary, Robert Falcon Scott and David Livingstone all have something to tell us about performance counselling. In 1953, Hillary, with the Sherpa Tenzing Norgay, was the first to conquer Everest. They were members of Sir John Hunt's British Everest expedition. It was a glorious occasion for which Hillary was knighted. But it concealed the fact it was the expedition's eighth attempt to fulfil their goal.

The lesson for counselling is don't give up when you think you are getting nowhere. Instead continue to reach out to people who need to get beyond the limitations of their roles. When you do you will reach your own summits with them, and you will achieve your own Everests in counselling.

Scott epitomizes another aspect of performance counselling – courage and perseverance. He was the English Antarctic explorer and leader of the ill-fated expedition to the South Pole. The weather got rough on the final stages but they carried on. They took only one sledge of supplies at this late stage of the expedition. Trekking the final 950 miles in two and half months they were met with bitter disappointment when they reached the South Pole on 18 January 1912: Amundsen's flag was already there. The Norwegians had got there first. By now Scott's party were suffering from scurvy, frost-bite, ravenous hunger and burgeoning blizzards. It was under these terrible conditions they began the return journey – a grim and fatal two-month trip that ended in tragedy. Scott and his compatriots died in their blizzard-bound tent. Scott collaborated with his colleagues and achieved their goal: reaching the South Pole.

In counselling we achieve our goals with people – but sometimes it takes great courage and determination. It can also be, on occasion, a time when great sacrifices have to be made by the manager and those persons in counselling.

Finally, it also has to be said that performance counselling can have its disappointments. Like exploring in the Antarctic we can have achievements but we can also experience disappointments. It is, however, better to have tried the collaborative approach to counselling than never to have bothered at all. Nothing worthwhile is achieved without some risk to ourselves or those engaged in counselling others.

The performance counselling lesson Livingstone gives us is an encouraging and inspiring one. David Livingstone was a great Scottish missionary. As a result of his safaris and explorations in the Zambezi and in pursuit of the source of the Nile he mapped out thousands of square miles of Africa south of the Equator. His maps, journals and books opened up a new world for other missionaries, explorers and those fighting against the slave trade. He never discovered the source of the Nile, yet he spent 30 years trying to find it. During this time he discovered all sorts of other places: Victoria Falls, the Zambezi and Lake Nyasa, for instance. Wonderful discoveries on his lifelong journey to find the source of the Nile.

Livingstone's example provides us with three further great insights into performance counselling. First of all, when you work with people in counselling you might not reach all of your goals. Second, that is no reason for giving up on them. And third – and very important – you discover many other skills, abilities and resources in the person that you never knew were there. Counselling in this sense is similar to going on a safari. It's a journey you take having faith in the person you are working with and being prepared for some surprises along the way. It's what Carl Rogers, the guru for many counsellors, has observed as the discovering of the individual's innate ability to solve their own problems. Next time you hear any stories about Hillary, Scott and Livingstone, remember what they have to teach us about counselling.

Person to person: a new agenda for managers

The new agenda for managers is a person-to-person one. This means getting beyond the role limitations imposed on employees by many organizations. When managers can get beyond the masks of the players at work, when they can scrap the stultified scripts of role players, when they can truly reach the person behind the role they play at work, then they will be able to start mining the gold within.

Assignments

1. Get together with your work group or team and map out the advantages and limitations of your roles at work. Pay particular attention to what *your* specific role allows you to do and prevents *you* from doing things that need to be done. Once you have done this share and compare what you have found and explore ways in which *you* can change your roles or how you occupy them.

2. Now go beyond those roles. Get behind the masks that everybody wears at work and make the effort to find out something significant about each other that you never knew before today. Be prepared to be surprised. Each person should make a statement to the group or in a pair. Begin each statement by saying:

One thing that you don't know about me and I am particularly good at is: 👌...
....
....
....
....

3. Now examine the crossed communications that exist amongst yourselves. How do these manifest themselves at work/in your personal lives? Have fun doing this. There are lots of comedy situations that rely on crossed communications, so join the club. Spell out the crossed communications you have with each other and keep track of where they occur and with whom and in what circumstances.

4. OK, now get serious. How are you going to uncross these communications you have with other people? Decide how you are going to do it. When you have done this set up a counselling session and try it out. You can vary it to suit your situation at work but try it this way first. Select an incident or series of incidents where you have got crossed communications with a person or group. Specify what goes wrong and say how you are going to put it right. Now role-play the situation with your group or another person. Do it as if you really meant it – as if it were happening to you *now*. OK, so what happened? Did you get crossed?. Where did it get tangled up? How did you manage to uncross the communications? Are you sure? How did you know? Were your communications in alignment? For how long? Congratulate yourself for doing so well. At least you know what you have to work on for next time.

5. How ready are you to risk collaborating with people to achieve the changes they need to make in their working lives? If you're not ready then find out what is stopping you and enrol in a counselling course for growing your own people. You *are* ready? Great. Start your exploring today. Become excited about what you can discover on your expedition. Cash in on the courage you have and reach people. Get beyond their roles and yours. Find out what untapped resources are there and mine the treasure within. Rub your Aladdin's lamp. Prove you're ready and make your day. Keep a record of how you have changed in the way you communicate with people, and do one other thing too – keep a record of how they behave differently towards you. Enjoy what you discover.

6

THE FUTURE STARTS NOW

'Knowing what to do and doing it are two separate steps. It takes time until you are strong in the new and have gone the complete shift. Until then, you must be vigilant in your efforts to change.' *Louise L. Hay*

Back-to-front managing

Have you ever thought what it would be like doing everything we do in life back to front? Imagine a world where you did the last thing first every time you wanted something done. You pay in the supermarket and then do your shopping. You eat your meals back to front. You start in the office and work your way back home. You get undressed to go out. You welcome people to parties by saying goodbye and walk upstairs backwards into your house. You play a round of golf by first sitting down and deciding on your scores and then go straight to the putting green and after that back down the fairways and to the tees until you have done this all the way from the 18th hole back to the first tee and then you come off the course. All this would be a bit strange and baffling wouldn't it? Life would be like one endless confusing series of video films running backwards towards the beginning of each event. Now, a question: what would be the point in all of this back-to-front, last-to-first activity? If you said none, absolutely none, you would be right. You can see there are some very significant and serious lessons to be learned from these trivial examples.

The first is probably obvious to you. Things work better and make more sense doing them front to back. Events have a sequence; they may not always unfold in a precise and predictable order, but they do have order and their meaning is understood. Secondly, working by beginning at the beginning and going through to the end can be better understood by other people as well as ourselves.

The third lesson may be one that hurts, but managers should be very wary of it. We can, over time, fall into the habit of becoming a 'back-to-front' manager – a manager who simply 'disciplines' a person without explaining or summarizing how the disciplinary interview came about is back-to-front managing. A manager who realizes an employee is having personal problems and who demands to know what their problem is without first checking to find out if the person is ready to tell their story, and in their own time, or change in their own way, is back-to-front managing. A manager who announces to his staff what has to be achieved without any attempt at explaining why it is in their interests to do it or how it will benefit the business is a back-to-front manager. These are all examples of back-to-front managing. We all have our own stories and examples of back-to-front managing that capture the quality of how managers try to get things done through other people.

Stop for a moment now and recall some of your own experiences of back-to-front managing. These may be things you have done yourself that you can talk about and have learned from. They can also be about back-to-front managing you have observed in your own organization or experienced through other managers. Reflect for a moment on what you have learned about back-to-front managing from these events. The chances are you will find them amusing and sometimes hysterically funny.

Above all this, you may have noticed something else. Managers who empower others know how to be, and are, front-to-back managers. They know how to begin at the beginning and build powerful relationships with people at work. These front-to-back managers are not simply interested in personal power; they live and perform in the bigger world of empowering others. They have discovered what it is to be green-fingered managers. They know how to nurture, grow and empower other people. It is their personal empowerment style when they are interacting with other people that will determine how much people will follow them, emulate them and develop themselves in the process.

Turning green-fingered

It is your personal empowerment style that determines how green-fingered you are as a manager. Personal empowerment of others depends on the style and quality of your interaction with others at work. We can all think of managers who seem to be able to build successful teams, lead others out of trouble and into successful performances at work, and inspire loyalty from people at work. Most of us also don't have to think too hard to recall managers who, instead of empowering others at work, engender a climate of distrust, hatred and envy against them. Trying to work out why these managers have become like this is a waste of time. Why? Well maybe it was because they saw other managers doing the same and they got rewarded for it. Or maybe they went to a business seminar and learned that was the way they were supposed to manage other people. Or it may even be that it was in their genes and they were just born nasty cusses. Who really cares about why they have become the way they are? Something more important really matters. It is not the 'why' question but the 'what' question: what is it about their personal style that makes one manager able to empower and inspire other people to greater heights or to overcome their self-imposed limitations and personal problems that may interfere with their performance at work?

The secret of style

There is a superb story that tells us about how important personal style is in becoming a green-fingered manager. A famous female French fashion designer was once interviewed by an American TV presenter at the end of her long and successful career. The interviewer had prepared very carefully for the interview. He had painstakingly researched all of the designs she had created over the years. He also worked hard at finding out what their countries of origin were and where the materials that went to make up the fabulous fashions came from.

After many months of background study and becoming familiar with the rise to stardom of this fashion designer and considering why so many people bought her designs, he was ready for the interview. During the interview, it suddenly occurred to him that something was missing. After all, anyone could have fashioned these designs. So he decided to ask *what* it was that made the difference. How could it be that after all these years she had never gone out of fashion? Without hesitation she replied she had never been in fashion but she had never, ever been out of style.

Her reply inspired the interviewer and changed the course of the whole interview. The interviewer completely forgot all of the parochial and predictable questions he had prepared for the interview. He also abandoned his pretentious knowledge and boring technical talk about the designs and materials. Instead he conducted a spontaneous live interview that revealed the rich and enchanting life of the designer and how her style came from her deep need to reach and understand other people. And this she expressed through the designs in her life's work which people wore and talked about from one generation to the next. Her designs and patterns were a metaphor for her personal style. All of those woven fabrics and bright colours and subtle blends and combinations of ideas were her statement of her inner self. Her style was the visible expression of this and this is why she was not a fashion freak. Fashion freaks come and go, but personal style – that has more electrifying power in it than the whole of the national power grid put together!

Empowering others – knowing your personal style

Managers have a clear-cut choice in choosing to empower others. They either become fashion-freak managers or they can tap into their personal style and empower others. Which do you prefer? Fashion-freak managers are all around us. They will always know about the latest fashion in managing others. But what they don't know is what their personal style is for empowering others. These managers will never be green-fingered managers. The nearest they will get to being green-fingered is adopting 'flavour of the month' approaches to managing. They are the instant experts on managing who simply don't know how they can use *their* personal style to empowers others to provide winning performances at work. These are the 'technique' generation of managers – managers brought up on a diet of fashion and starved of style.

The fickleness of fashion is like the Rubik cubes that came and went out of fashion. You can copy the solution and produce it, and show off to your friends, but as soon as you have worked out the solution along comes the Snake, another problem-solving invention that tortures our minds until we have solved the puzzle. Finding our personal style is different. It is a bit like understanding ourselves, and to do that we need to know what aspects of our personal style work for us and which bits we need to wrestle with until we get the kinds of results with people we wish to empower. Once we discover what our preferred personal empowerment style is, we can then begin to use it. If you don't use it, you lose it.

It is in the using of your personal empowerment style that you can consciously see, feel and hear people saying how it affects them. People react to each other; it is unavoidable. Our personal style can imprison people or release the process of change within them. When we are in contact with other people, they react to our personal style. Richard Bandler, a psychologist who has empowered millions of people and inspired change in their lives, was reported as saying, 'People seem to spend more time figuring out how a washing machine works than how to run their own brain.'

Just think what running your own brain can do for you. For one thing, you can make the most of your personal empowerment style and for another you can choose to adopt an appropriate personal empowerment style for any situation you find yourself in with other people. Not only will you be able to nurture and grow people: you will be able to utilize different empowerment styles to bring out the best in their personal performance at work.

Personal empowerment styles

Studies of how people use their personal styles have revealed five main styles that are significantly related to personal empowerment and performance counselling at work. The main styles are:

- The probing style
- The revealing style
- The interpreting style
- The supporting style
- The evaluating style

The way each style or combination of styles is adopted by managers can empower or disempower people at work.

The probing style

A manager with a probing style is always looking for something – picking and poking and uncovering. They are a bit like an intelligent precocious child – with the penetrating curiosity of a budding detective. They love asking questions. Lots of them. They are what I call the Sherlock Holmes managers. They engage in what can be called inquisitions. They care about people but they are bent on helping others by unearthing information and challenging unchallenged assumptions. Questions, questions and yet more questions characterizes their style of trying to empower others.

Now sometimes their questions will make all the difference to their digging and they will discover new and vital information that provides people with a fresh perspective and purpose as well as a new direction in which to solve their personal or work-related problems. But at other times this probing style will deter people from finding their own solutions to their problems and inhibit their personal satisfaction and demotivate them at work. They will have transformed the power of questioning into hostile interrogation. These are the 'terrorist' managers. They disempower people and savage their hopes and aspirations and will to work. Probing can be empowering and help people discover useful information about themselves or it can be paralysing and destroy their competence, their belief in themselves and cripple their confidence to perform well at work.

At best the probing style provides essential information that people need or have to find in order to overcome their problems. Without it they are stuck in their problem and their performance can continue to be adversely affected at work. At worst, the probing style can deteriorate into a careless and cruel interrogation of others – a misguided attempt by the manager to 'get to the root of the problem at all costs'.

The revealing style

Another typical style managers can use to empower others is the revealing style. When managers use the revealing style to empower others they are attempting to understand the other person. So instead of probing they are more interested in finding out if they understand what the person thinks and feels and considers their problem to be. And they want to understand what the person intends doing about their problem and how they might overcome their performance difficulties at work.

The revealing style of personal empowerment is clearly characterized by three forms of understanding. First, the manager is genuinely interested in understanding the person in counselling. Second, the manager is interested in finding out if people understand themselves and the problems they are facing. Third, the manager using the revealing style is interested in understanding how far they share the view of any particular issue or problem or solution to a problem by the person in counselling.

When we use the revealing style and adhere to being interested and understanding the person, the problems and their solutions in this way, it works well. Solutions to personal and performance problems may not always be obvious or immediate. Managers using the revealing style of personal empowerment overcome this and tenaciously avoid the hidden agendas and the pitfalls of quick-fix formulas found in many aspects of managing. Remember this, the revealing style of personal empowerment is about revealing: revealing the person to themselves in such a way that they can take purposeful action to solve their real or apparent problems.

The revealing style works best when the manager acts like a mirror – holding it up to the person in performance counselling at work. In doing so, the person sees themselves clearer and so does the manager. This, then, can form the basis for any personal insight or changes in performance the person may need to make in their lives or at work. This is when the revealing style works best. When it does not, managers typically are only interested in their own agendas, their own reflections, and their own understanding of events. These managers are concealers. They are using a concealing style of managing, and this stultifies and inhibits the release of fresh hope, vibrant energy, renewed problem-solving and personal enthusiasm to work. Concealers may mean well but are lost to the notion that they understand others best and the solutions to their work-related problems better than the persons do themselves. Concealers conceal and revealers reveal. Which are you? Which do you prefer? Why?

The interpreting style

The interpreting style of empowering others relies on the manager playing the role of the expert. Managers adopting this style of empowerment assume they have the solutions to personal and performance-related problems at work. All that is necessary is for the person to describe their problem and the manager interprets what is wrong and how to put it right.

This style of empowerment works better with 'things' than it does with people. It has a great deal to offer in rectifying technical problems and machine malfunctions. The problem is described, analysed and a course of action taken to solve it. Managers engaging in the interpreting style are relied on for their technical knowledge. At best they are master technicians, masters of interpreting when things go wrong and how they can put them right. But when they adopt this approach with people, they are not so effective. Their attempts at interpreting what people are thinking and feeling and what they should do to improve their performance at work or resolve personal problems can often add to problems rather than solve them. In its extreme form, the manager with this personal style interferes with a person's ability to perform at work.

Yet there are times when the interpreting style of empowerment can make a major difference to people, their motivation, how they see themselves and how they perform at work. What makes the difference? The difference lies in not trying to tell those in performance counselling how they should solve their problems or what they ought to do if they are to overcome personal difficulties in their private lives that are interfering with their performance at work. The wisdom of using the interpreting style to deal with people problems can best be illustrated by a short story about a wise green-fingered manager.

The bird in the hand

A clever old worker called Frank spent a lot of time testing out the managers at his job. He used to spring surprises and loved putting questions to them. Often he would dream up a riddle or pose some curious conundrum and he would then ask them to interpret what the problem was and how he should solve it. He loved doing this because he put the managers 'on the spot' and he would see them take the bait that he had dangled before them just like he did when he went fishing. The bait was often taken by the managers and sometimes they would be right, but most of the time they would get embarrassed and make real fools of themselves. This happened because Frank nearly always had a different answer from the one given by the managers.

One day a new manager arrived. Frank dreamt up this test for him: he would go to him with a tiny bird in his hand and ask what it was he had in his hand. To entice the manager he would open one of his fingers to let the manager see some of the bird's feathers. This would be the bait. Once the manager said he had a bird in his hand Frank would ask if it was alive or dead. If the manager said it was alive, Frank would crush it and say it was dead and that he had no confidence in the manager. If the manager said it was dead, Frank would open his hands and let the bird fly away and then say he had no confidence in the manager. Old Frank was really excited and thrilled at the prospect of catching out another 'know-all' manager. Either way he could not fail. His plan was foolproof.

So what happened? Frank timed his surprise to coincide with the new manager meeting the 20 other people at a welcoming party in his department. He came up to him and said, 'How do you do, they call me Frank around here. They say you are a fair manager and are good at helping folks at work to solve their problems. Well I've got a right handful here.' As he said this he held up his cupped hands to the manager and let one of his fingers open very slightly – just enough to show the feathers of the bird. 'First of all, what I want to know is this. What is it I've got in my hands?' Right away the manager said 'Well, Frank, I suppose you and I both know it is a bird. Is that right?' 'You're damn right... it is a bird. But tell me now, is the bird dead or is it alive?' The manager paused thoughtfully, looked at Frank, and then carefully said, 'I think the answer to that lies in your hands, Frank, does it not?' Frank smiled ruefully, and replied in a somewhat astonished tone, 'My my, it is true what they say about you. You really are fair and you do know how to help people at work.' From that day on Frank never played any more pranks with managers. Instead he spent many hours telling the story about the bird in the hand and the wisest manager he had ever met.

The supporting style

Another approach the green-fingered manager can adopt is the supporting style of managing others. The supporting style is exemplified best by managers who are emphatically oriented towards 'backing up' those for whom they are responsible. At best this style communicates caring and acceptance of people at work and their limitations as well as their personal capabilities. At worst, the supporting style is uncritical, obsequious and preoccupied with creating circumstances that are agreeable to others no matter what the cost to the organization.

One manager captured this view when he said to me, 'This organization is run for the benefit of the staff, not the customers – you must remember this if you are to understand how things get done here.' But things can be different! Another manager who adopted and encouraged others through his supportive style simply described how he did it and why people seemed to be much more animated, motivated and adventurous in his part of the organization. 'It's like this: people know they can take risks because I am there to support them. I may not always agree with them but I respect their right to prove me wrong. I am the safety net and they know it.'

Safety nets and the circus

I like the idea of the supporting style being like a safety net. It reminds me of the great flying trapeze artistes. When they first begin to use the trapeze they are strapped in and harnessed and protected from damaging themselves. Because they know this they overcome their fears and are able to perform breathtaking performances and further develop their abilities. It doesn't end here, though. When the harness is taken away they still have a safety net – just in case they need it. Just imagine you are watching a great trapeze artiste: what do you see? Do they keep falling off the trapeze? Are they constantly checking the net? Are they unwilling to climb up to the trapeze? Do they refuse to 'fly' across the circus arena at the moment when they must leave the trapeze? No. The chances are you will see someone performing with complete confidence – as if there was no net there at all.

There is an important lesson in empowering people that we we can all learn from circus trapeze performers. Feeling supported helps people to overcome their fears. The confidence that flows from being supported by something or someone has another important conse-quence: people eventually perform as if they are not supported or at least perform in a way where they appear not to need the support that is offered to them. Now that really is personal empowerment at work.

But let's be clear on one point: the supporting style is not aimed at creating dependency in others. Dependency only creates compliance and stultifies human initiative and effort. A business dies the day it starts to engender dependency in its employees.

The supporting style works best when people need and want autonomy in their jobs, and at the same time know they have the support of their manager. Like the high flyers in the circus, though, they may think they do not need the support, but it is there in the background, ready for them should they need it. Do you recognize the supporting style? Is it part of your style or your colleagues? What place does it have in your organization? You may also wonder just how supporting and empowering it is for people or how far it goes towards undermining them and creating dependency. You need to know where to draw the line while still getting the best out of using the supporting style to empower others.

The evaluating style

Many managers tend to use the evaluating style to empower others. These managers are the evaluators – the judges. They sincerely believe they know what is right and what is wrong. They are assured about the actions that need to be taken to get results. They know the issues in organizations and how they should be resolved and they let people know about it. And it is not just theory: much of it is based on their practical experience.

Evaluating managers will assess each situation and tell people how it should be tackled. Often they will be right – right that is in the sense that their judgement is sound. In some cases people will feel secure that a judgement has been made. They may also willingly take action based on the evaluating style of their manager. It would be a strange business where judgements were never made by managers. However, it is often the way managers make judgements that can inspire or demotivate and demoralize or breed resentment in those whom they manage. The judge may always be right but he is not always liked. Managers using the evaluating style in performance counselling at work would do well to remember the managerial leader Jean Richard Bloch's wise decree: 'Your actions shall be the judgement passed on your judgements.' So it is useful to remember that when we are using the evaluating style to make judgements about other people we also run the risk of being wrong.

A manager I knew in the oil industry who relied very heavily on the evaluating style once said: 'Every day I am making decisions – decisions based on my judgement of this business and the people in it. Judging things in this industry is sometimes difficult – but judging people, now that's a whole lot worse. I have climbed the career ladder well up until now with the motto Think, Judge, Act. But now I am working more often with people, not just technology, I need also to understand how and what they think about my judgement of the actions we should take. You don't have to do that with an oil pump.' This particular manager may have been hooked into his evaluating style but he was aware that there were times when it worked well for him and times when he was a victim of his over-reliance of judging the performance problems he faced with other people.

Upside and downside

Clearly there is an upside and a downside with all of the personal empowerment styles we may use as managers.

Probing versus interrogating

The manager who uses the probing style can often access critical information and produce desired solutions so that performance problems at work are overcome or at least alleviated. On the other hand, the probing style can just simply produce antagonism between people at work and their managers. One consequence of this is actually to withhold the information required because of the probing style being used by the manager. Here you need to ask yourself, 'When does probing become interrogation?'

Revealing versus concealing

The manager using the revealing style acts best to empower others when they show people they are working on hunches they have about them. Look around for these managers in your own organization. You will know them by the way they listen to people and act on their hunches. They make their hunches clear to people. They listen and then suggest to people at work what problems they face and how they might overcome them or at least manage their situation better. When they are on form these managers are listening beyond what is being said. They are 'listening with their third ear and seeing with their third eye'. A tell-tale sign of the revealing style is when the manager communicates to people at work what it is they seem to be trying to say, what they appear to be doing about their problems, and what the results might mean to them. Listen and look out for the revealing style.

The opposite of the revealing style is the concealing style. I have met many managers who use the concealing style with people and their performance problems at work. The concealing style is the hidden agenda – the style that does not reveal to the other person what the real issues are or the real problems they believe need to be resolved. Managers with the concealing style are so insecure that they are unable to be honest, direct or clear in the way they manage and try to achieve organizational objectives. The concealing managers are often summed up by the people they manage: 'We don't know where we stand with them, or where they are coming from.' There may be occasions when concealing information is appropriate. However, many managers fail to crawl out from behind the concealing approach to empowering others. I believe this is because they have got into the habit of concealing from people what really needs to be faced and tackled in their performance at work.

Interpreting versus blocking

The interpreting style for empowering others can often help people to improve their performance at work. With the interpreting style you get the best from people when you can say to them what you believe they are saying and what they are doing means to you. For example, when someone comes to you to discuss their problems and how they might improve their performance you would respond by saying something like, 'The way you are describing this problem sounds like' or 'You seem to be saying your efforts to manage this problem have been' or 'As I have been sitting here listening to you I have been wondering if one of the main problems you face is...?' Managers using this style put an emphasis on listening and new possibilities and suggesting people might change their thinking and behaviour. Blocking can put a rapid end to all of this personal empowerment activity. It cuts right through rapport and the sense of belonging and inclusion that you might have cultivated with people at work. Blocking strangles people's efforts at improving their performance or any fresh attempts at solving their performance-related problems at work.

When are we blocking? We block when we fail to respect or refuse to pursue our understanding of what the person is going through or the personal efforts they are taking to manage themselves at work. Examples of blocking are: when we say we can't help someone who needs help; when we refuse to give our understanding of the situation when it is asked for; when we tell someone to go and work things out for themselves when it is clear they are in desperate need of listening, understanding, leadership and guidance. In its best light, the interpreting style gives new hope and guidance to people at work. Blocking does the opposite. It cuts out hope and leaves people to drift, fending for themselves and not knowing which way to turn to resolve their performance problems.

Supporting versus withdrawing

Supporting style managers are there when we need them. Not suffocating or pushing, managers using the supporting style of empowerment send the signal to people that what they think and feel and how they behave at work really counts. The supporting style starts from the position of caring and encouragement. Green-fingered managers who use this style of empowerment at work 'back their people'.

I once asked an employee in the computer industry – which at the time was going through a rapid period of change and job losses – why he was so loyal to his boss. He said: 'He is with me all the way and I mean all the way. Now it is my turn to be with him – all the way to the wire.' Managers who use the supporting style to empower people at work are in turn supported by the people they manage. The supporting style breeds loyalty. These managers are with their people through 'thick and thin'.

What happens when managers can't or won't use the supportive style of personal empowerment? The withdrawal of the supporting style is clearly noticed by people at work. At first they may get frustrated and confused; then they get angry and resent being left to sort out their own problems. Withdrawing support from people at work is best illustrated by the now classic series of Hawthorne studies of performance at work. There were many aspects to the study but one theme stood out clearly above all: when people knew they were supported in what they were doing and there was interest in them, their output increased and they became happier and more satisfied with the work they were doing. Other studies strongly suggest that sickness absence can drop when managers show interest in and support people at work.

Evaluating versus ignoring

The evaluating style makes it possible for people at work to know what value managers put on their work performance. This may help people to be clear about what matters to their manager. However, it can make managers much less clear and even prevent them from knowing what matters to the people they are managing, which can be a big disadvantage.

Judgements about situations, and people at work are all fundamental to achieve the desired performance at work, but it is crucial to decide whose judgements will contribute to this improved performance. People who decide for themselves what they need to change in their performance at work and how it will be done and evaluated 'own' the problem. As a result they are more likely to be motivated to solving their personal and work-related problems. Managers who use the evaluating style in a heavy-handed way run the risk of being wrong in three ways when they 'judge' poor performance and how it should be rectified. First of all they may assume they know what the problem is and how the person can 'improve' – and be wrong. Second, they may judge the problem is not relevant when it is absolutely important to the person and their performance. Third, the solutions to improved performance may be very interesting to the manager but quite unworkable, irrelevant and inconsequential for those concerned about improving their personal performance at work. At worst the manager who engages in the evaluating style in this way achieves an undesirable goal; they quickly alienate people from their work and their manager. People are no longer involved. It is no longer their problem. When this happens people are no longer motivated to change. Managers who have become green-fingered realize this and discover that it is not so much the evaluating style itself which is the problem but the crude way many managers use it in their attempts to improve performance at work.

Here is one thing worse than using the evaluating style badly: that is not using it all – ignoring people at work and their problems. This is perhaps the biggest mistake any manager could make in managing people, themselves and their business. The ignoring manager is the 'head in the sand' manager. And there are still some of them about. Any left in your organization?

With a sense of purpose and perspective the evaluating style of empowering others can work and work well. But simply issuing statements, judgements and courses of action without 'taking the pulse' of the people affected by your judgements means dragging people along to improve their work performance. It may not be easier, but it is infinitely more appropriate to reach decisions and judgements, and obtain commitment to change, when the personal interests, preferences, and motivation of people are involved in their own performance counselling. They may struggle and you may struggle to make the germane judgements that lead to improved performance at work, but together you will make the decisions and take the actions and recognize the fears and feelings that need to be dealt with along the way. Remember, the person is part of the process of using the evaluating style to improve their performance. They are not simply there to be told what to do. When we assimilate this simple truth the evaluating style can become a powerful ally in performance counselling.

Spotting the personal empowerment styles

Building trust, belonging and using information to make choices are all related to personal styles of empowerment. Knowing the kinds of personal skills involved in the different personal empowerment styles gives the green-fingered manager a wider range of choices to deploy in performance counselling at work. See if you can spot the different styles used. Take a look at the samples here and check off which style is being used; then compare this with the style key at the end of this chapter. How accurate were you?

Personal empowerment styles

Write a P, R, I, S, or E, in each box indicating which style you believe is being used by the manager. (P=probing, R=revealing, I=interpreting, S=supporting, E=evaluating.)

1. It seems to me your drive for success overrides your need to be popular. [ ]

2. I like the way you handle customers. You are destined for the top in this business – just let me know if I can help you in any way. [ ]

3. As a woman, what difficulties do you foresee being a problem for you in this organization? [ ]

4. I am wondering how far you are confusing having a good education with being a good manager of people at work and what you feel about it. [ ]

5. If you take that attitude, it will make you very unpopular here – that's not how we do things in this company. [ ]

6. Why do you think you were not a success with the project? I am interested in what you mean by success. [ ]

7. You need to argue your corner forcefully – I will send you a list of the main points to make and how you can put them over. [ ]

8. What specific efforts have you made to take responsibility and who was this with and what results did it produce? [ ]

9. What you need is friends. Moving from one place to another you lose friends you make others. I would say that what you need is to get out there and meet people – as many as you can. Things will soon get better. [ ]

10. I wonder if you are just getting paranoid and anxious about your future. With all the job losses – you could be uncertain about paying your bills and it may be is affecting your home life. [ ]

Now get to know your own personal empowerment style and practise the others. What suits you best? Which combinations work? Which do not? How specifically do people react to your use of these types of personal empowerment skills? How does the way you are using them make it possible for them to change their thinking, the way they feel and their behaviour at work?

Applying your personal empowerment style at work

Don't ask what is right or wrong but ask what is appropriate. The great artist Picasso is rumoured to have been asked by a conscientious art student if it was right or wrong to adhere to a particular school of painting. Picasso is supposed to have said that nothing is right or wrong in art and expression in art was about what was appropriate – what seems right at the time.

This story has a lesson for green-fingered managers. It is simple yet clear. If we doggedly cling to what is the right or wrong way of managing people we run the risk of enslaving them, frustrating and freezing their abilities – not empowering them. It is clearly implicit in managing people at work that our intent is to get the best out of them. The paradox is, however, that we often fail to do this because of the narrow range of personal empowerment styles we use to help people to perform well at work and feel good about themselves. Like the art student, we become preoccupied with the 'right' or 'wrong' way of doing things. The only difference is that we are working with people instead of paint. To motivate people and achieve organizational goals, the green-fingered manager does what is appropriate – what seems right at the time, for that person, their work, their personal concerns and being valued for the performance they put into their work.

The green-fingered manager remembers to nurture and grow and value the people who provide the performances that help to make the business a success. The naive manager simply clings to what is right and wrong – whether or not it improves performance at work. The green-fingered manager is the artist. The naive manager is still the student. One holds the keys to empowering people at work the other just fiddles with the lock.

Assignment

Think about this assignment very carefully and consider these questions:

1. How green-fingered are you as a manager?

2. What is your personal empowerment style?

3. Is it personal to you?

4. How far do you create conditions at work where other people trust you?

5. What evidence do you have that you are able to empower people at work to overcome their frustrations and disappointments?

6. How much does your personal empowerment style contribute to people becoming genuinely motivated to achieve agreed performance goals?

7. Which abilities have people developed through the increased confidence they have gained as a result of your personal empowerment style?

8. How strongly do the people you counsel at work believe that what they say and do at work is important and that you genuinely appreciate them?

9. In your absence, how confident are you in the people you counsel and their performance at work?

10. How would the people you counsel at work have perceived these questions about you and what are the answers they would have given?

Write your answers down and then ask the same questions of the people you counsel at work, e.g. colleagues, members of your team, co-workers, office staff and anyone you supervise or conduct appraisals with in your organization.

Answers to personal empowerment style questionnaire
(P=probing, R=revealing, I=interpreting, S=supporting, E=evaluating.)

1=I, 2=S, 3=P, 4=R, 5=E, 6=R, 7=S, 8=P, 9=E, 10=I.

How well did you recognize the different personal empowerment styles? Share and compare your scores with someone you trust and respect. Ask them for honest feedback on your scores and what they think about them.

Make a list of the personal empowerment styles you feel most comfortable, confident and competent to use and the situations in which you find yourself using them. Analyse the benefits and the costs of using these styles to yourself and for others.

Now produce a personal action plan specifying those personal empowerment styles which you wish to introduce more into your work, how you will do it, when it will be achieved and how you will know you are using these new styles.

Finally, set a review date to assess how successful you have been in carrying out your personal action plan and what results it has had for your performance and the effects it has had on people at work.

7

TURNING POINT – PUTTING PERSONAL EMPOWERMENT INTO PRACTICE

'I become what I choose and I choose what I become.' *Will Schultz*

Getting started

The first thing you need to do as a green-fingered manager is to turn what you know about personal empowerment into action. So what do you do? You practise what you preach and preach what you practise. To start being a green-fingered manager you must take putting personal empowerment into action seriously. You know that people at work respond enthusiastically and energetically when they are personally valued. You believe in prizing people and caring for them as persons and not just as bodies occupying roles that have to be filled for the organization to function and survive. You realize that people at work need to belong and identify with their organization. And you want to encourage their association, affiliation and affection for each other. All this knowing, believing and encouraging will come to nought, however, unless you use the personal empowerment styles that make it possible for people at work to take action – action on their problems, action on the solutions that matter to them, and action on taking responsibility for their own performance at work.

Personal empowerment at work requires managers to be green-fingered. Sowing the seeds of encouragement and nurturing the growth of people at work takes patience, practice and time. Reaping the harvest of your efforts will be seen in the personal responsibility people at work take for themselves and the improved quality of their working relationships. The going may get tough and you may feel like giving up along the way. After all, it is so much easier to fall back onto our old and comforting habits. And it may seem easier to rely on heavy-handed managing – indeed, it may be easier – but it shuts the door on personal empowerment. If we take the apparently easy way of using our old habits we shall suffer the longer-term consequences of poor performance, demotivated people and an alienated workforce. Becoming a green-fingered manager means making a personal commitment to overcome and break our bad habits of managing that limit people at work.

New habits for old

All this sounds easy, and for some people it is. They simply describe the new habits they are going to put into practice with people at work and then they do it. But many managers find it difficult to give up their old habits. Like the time-tested saying, their old habits die hard.

Dr Chris Argyris, the American organizational and management consultant at Harvard, has found this out through his work with clients such as General Electric, Shell Oil, Polaroid, General Foods, IBM and Dupont. Many managers can describe the new habits they want to adopt and the way in which they will conduct personal interactions with people at work. They even specify what they will say, how they say it and the kinds of listening, questioning and personal empowerment styles they will deploy in their working contact with people. Now what happens is fascinating and of great interest to anyone who wants to be a green-fingered manager. Instead of introducing their new habits, they simply carry on in the same old way! I have found this in my own work in the food industry, and also in the computer industry with Japanese and American-based computer firms.

So culture is not the key. It is habit. Many managers are prisoners of their own habits; it is their habits of managing people that need to be changed if they are to reap the benefits of being a green-fingered manager. Curiously, many newly recruited managers and mature managers do the same thing. They agree there is a need for nurturing, growing and prizing people. They agree they need to reach the whole person and not just respond to them like a role player or someone who has a small bit-part in their organization. Moreover, they even agree that they will change their personal empowerment styles to suit the situation and the person they are managing. And, yes, they also agree that they will stop behaving and thinking preconceived perceptions of people at work.

In other words, they say they will stop their bad habits and replace them with new and desirable ones. Wouldn't managing people, empowering them and making the most of performance counselling at work be an easy task if it was as simple as that? Chris Argyris discovered a simple but profound truth in his work on strategic change in organizations: people do not do what they say they will do! In other words, where change is concerned we are inclined to say one thing and do another.

Espoused theory and theory in use

Argyris noticed managers have an espoused theory and a theory they put to use. I understand the espoused theory of managers to be the thoughts, conceptualizations, brainstormings and the creative possibilities, language and behaviour they say they will use in the way they manage people at work. I would go further than this and say that the espoused theory of managers is the way they say and assume they manage others. Now here is the interesting part: for many managers it is not how they actually manage people at all. They are managers who are stuck – stuck in their old habits of managing, stuck in antiquated beliefs about how to manage people at work, and stuck in the way they translate new learning about managing people at work and their performance into practice.

If you are serious about changing and becoming a green-fingered manager you need to ask yourself a fundamental question: What must I do to be able to cross the bridge from my espoused theory and make it into my theory in use or action?

A satisfactory answer to this question will make it possible for you to use a wider range of personal empowerment styles with people at work. It can also unlock the doors of communication and unblock your own future potential as well as those you manage. If you don't change, then neither will the people you manage at work. Instead of your performance counselling sessions with people being productive, renewing, invigorating and reaching the whole person, they will simply be rituals that frustrate them and imprison their potential and motivation for work. When you change, they change. There is hope, there is a future – and people at work need to know this. Hope and faith in the future are essential to people at work. Without these two pillars of perception people often lose the will to work.

Defensive mechanisms and defensive routines

It is important for us to recognize our own defensive mechanisms and how these prevent us from empowering others and their performance. When our defensive mechanisms come into play they lead us into playing out defensive routines with people at work. Many a true word was spoken by the manager in the computer industry who told me he could empower people if only he could stop 'spitting in his own soup'. He kept getting in his own way. When I asked him what he meant by this, he said that he had good intentions; he set out to develop rapport using the information that was important to the person in performance counselling and create a climate of care, where the feelings of belongingness and affiliation could flourish. He earnestly, honestly and urgently wanted to reach the whole person and he was convinced it was the right way to empower and manage people and their performance at work. His personal pronouncements were laudable and honourable. He meant well. But, there was a but: in practice, he did the same things he had done so many times before in managing people at work. He finished sentences for people; he assumed that he knew all the answers to the performance problems they experienced at work; he played the expert; he conveyed a sense of remoteness from the people he managed; he habitually discouraged affiliation, association and affection between himself and others at work. And he did not really listen to people and their views, thoughts and feelings about how they might overcome their performance problems, or at least better manage them. A clear case of his espoused theory being overwhelmed by his theory in use. He automatically exercised his defensive routines and these prevented him from making the real and valid changes he so fervently wanted to make in his performance counselling with people at work. After four hard working sessions with me he began to identify the defensive routines he was using and started making the changes in himself that would lead to real empowerment of others at work.

Deciding to change and changing

Changing takes time. But it also requires us to make a decision to change. What changes do you wish to make? These may be changes in your personal empowerment style, changes in the way you try to build nurturing relationships with people at work, or they may simply be more subtle changes such as the way you listen to people and their concerns about personal and performance-related problems.

Capture the decisions and the changes you have decided to make that will free you to empower people at work. Write them down *now*. Make it clear what it is you will actually do. How will you be feeling when you put those changes into practice in yourself and with others? Be honest with yourself. Be as specific as you can. When will you start making these changes? How will it look to others? How will you know when you have achieved those changes you say you have decided to make in managing others at work?

Now stop for a moment and review your decisions and the changes you say you will be making. Any reservations? If you have, go back over your decisions and be satisfied about what you have decided and the changes you will put into practice with people at work. Don't proceed with any changes until you feel completely committed to the decisions you have made. Ready? OK, now you can start replacing your unwanted habits of managing in the dustbin of history and let your new choices and changes express themselves in managing people at work.

Turning point

Congratulations, you have reached your personal turning point. You have decided on the changes you need to make to become a green-fingered manager. When you have done this, and can do it, you have negotiated and agreed a personal empowerment contract with your-self.

Be vigilant about those unwanted old bad habits of managing people. Look out for them. They sometimes have a tendency to come creeping back when you least expect them or want them. If, or when, they do, don't give up. This is a crucial part of your turning point. Turning back now means surrendering to your old unwanted manager-ial habits. Surrendering to them renders you a victim. If you allow this to happen, you are not managing yourself – your habits are managing you. This is the precise time when you need to keep your decisions in mind and continue with the changes you are making in managing.

Sometimes you will find it helps to form an alliance with a colleague or someone whom you trust to give you feedback on the changes you are making in how you empower people at work. When you feel confident enough, you can also ask those people who come to you for performance counselling to give you their views, thoughts and feelings about how they perceive your way of managing them. When this works well it is a tremendous confirmation that you are on the right track and have not only reached the turning point in becoming a green-fingered manager but gone further and begun to reap the benefits of using our new-found styles to empower people at work.

The green-fingered manager at work

Now you are ready to put the green-fingered approach to empowering people to work. But before you do, let's look below at some examples of the way managers have conducted personal performance counselling sessions with people at work.

Spotting the green-fingered manager

Here are some examples of managers faced with difficult situations with people at work. Which ones do you identify with? Which examples are evidence of the green-fingered manager at work? Which ones are not green-fingered managers? Why? Why not? See if you can spot the difference in the styles and skills used by these managers, and say which examples show the manager empowering others at work, and those restricting and inhibiting personal solutions, and employee efforts and motivation.

Example 1

Derek – a 49-year-old married man with two teenage daughters being told he is redundant from an engineering firm.

Manager. Well, Derek, sit down. I have bad news for you.

Derek. Yes, I can guess what's coming. It's typical of this firm: nobody wants to know you after you're 45.

Manager. It's worse than that, Derek. The truth is you are surplus to requirements. You have been a drain on the business and we're making you redundant right away. There is a more than generous redundancy package. Sylvia will spell it out for you – it is all very simple. Now I expect you to have your desk cleared by tomorrow.

Derek. I don't believe I'm hearing this – it's some kind of sick joke. I know more about this business than anybody else and you are kicking me out. I'm... I'm so bloody angry.

Manager. That's another thing, Derek, you are too emotional as a person – you can't expect good references if you behave like that. I have said what I have to say – you can wind everything else up with Salaries next week and Sylvia will see to the rest of the detail. Now I think I have made myself perfectly clear – any questions, Derek?

Derek. Only one – how do prats like you get where they are and still keep a job? (Derek then sits in smouldering silence for a while – hate written all over his face). I'm never going to forget what happened today, never. I'm stunned and I feel sick – I don't know what to do next... It's the end of a life... the end of the line.

Example 2

A 33-year-old man – single parent with a 12-year-old daughter called Michelle – has just found out from 'someone in the office' that he is to be made redundant.

Manager. Gary I heard that you wanted to see me urgently so I rang you right away – come in and please sit down. Now what seems to be concerning you so much?

Gary. You damn well know what it's about – I'm boiling angry at you – and finding out the way I did. I have no job to come to after next Monday... I'm seething. I feel so mad. I could hit somebody. It is your fault; you promised me my job was safe. I found out from the office last night – me and twenty others are for the chop... the end of this week. If I had got hold of you last night I would have killed you or done something I'd regret. You have let us down badly.

Manager. I'm sure you have a good reason to be angry, Gary, and I would be angry too thinking I might be losing my job – especially if I found out the way you did. You must be feeling really annoyed with me – thinking the way you do right now.

Gary. You are damned right – I am mad at you. It was you, wasn't it?

You set it up – you... to put me on the scrap heap and elbow me out of the department.

Manager. I wonder how you came to that conclusion, Gary?

Gary. Well, everybody knows the firm is having a hard time and the last to join the company are the first to be made redundant.

Manager. And you believe that you are one of the last to join and the first to go?

Gary. Yeah... I do.

Manager. I want you to listen very carefully to what I have to say. Our business is suffering and recently we have had some difficulties in getting orders for the factory. That much is true.

Gary. So I'm going to lose my job at the end of the week?

Manager. I wish you had asked me that question sooner, Gary – but I am glad you asked me it now. Gary, I can tell you now your job will be there for you next week.

Gary. So my job is safe... for the moment.

Manager. Yes, your job is safe for the moment.

Gary. I feel such a fool now... listening to all that gossip from the office. What I'm... I'm really worried about is looking after Michelle, paying the mortgage and settling the bills for the car... I suppose I need to know that my job is safe.

Manager. I'm glad we could clarify that your job is safe and that you could tell me how you feel and come to me with your concerns about your job. Gary, I wonder if you could help me... how do you think we could deal with situations like this differently in the future?

Gary. Well, to be honest, I guess I would like to come direct to you and talk them out and decide what the position is, then...

Manager. Then we could avoid relying on the office gossip as a source of information that we just have to sort out and untangle to get to the core of the problem.

Gary. I agree – but I would want to think it over. There are quite a few things I know can be improved on and I've got some thoughts for getting to grips with the problem of getting new orders.

Manager. That's great, Gary. If you could give some more thought to the kinds of problems we need to face together – I would appreciate it. Gary, I'd like us to set a specific time aside for this... let's do that now.

Gary. Fine by me... and thanks for listening.

Example 3

Rachel, single and a 23-year-old newly recruited graduate into the confectionery industry as a trainee manager at a meeting with her manager.

Rachel. These people I am working with, they just seem to be unable to think at my level. I spend so much explaining to them and still they can't understand what I want them to do... and those times they do understand I have to be on their backs making sure they are doing it and doing it right. You would have thought getting and keeping the flow and quality of the chocolate is a simple enough job... sometimes I think I am dealing with a bunch of brainless idiots!

Manager. Rachel, I want to make sure I understand you here. You are saying you believe the people in your training section are stupid and are not motivated to produce quality work... is that right?

Rachel. I suppose I am saying that... it sounds awful... but, yes, that is what I am saying and I believe I am right.

Manager. Right Rachel, you are surrounded by these stupid people in your training section... So what would you like instead... them all to be brilliant?

Rachel. No, no, not brilliant... I'm not interested in sarcasm. I just want them to be able to be clear about what I expect from them and that they would go about their jobs and not have to be chased up, although I want them to be self-motivated and take personal responsibility for quality on the production line...

Manager. What specifically would you see and hear that would tell you 'these people are self-motivated and are taking personal responsibility on the line'... and how would this make you feel?

Rachel. I would see them carrying out the daily checks and pursuing their tasks on the line and each shift would hand over smoothly to the next and tell me how good they felt about taking charge of their job. There would less complaints and an increase in the percentage of high-quality runs on the chocolate slab lines. When I had all of that I would feel a sense of achievement... I'd feel good.

Manager. Your efforts would be appreciated and recognized.

Rachel. Yes – that's right. My position would be recognized.

Manager. Yes – recognized. By whom?

Rachel. What? By the people I am working with.

Manager. And I realize it is important for you to be recognized by the people you work with... on the chocolate line.

Rachel. You know I never realized what made me feel the way I did, but now I do... I need recognition for my efforts.

Manager. And the people you work with right now, I wonder what they need...

Rachel. Umm... The same thing. Yes they need to be recognized and valued for their efforts as well. Oh... I see what has happened... I think.

Manager. Yes – recognized and valued... Now looking at the difficulties you have described I am curious about the way you see these people now.

Rachel. I see that I haven't valued them or recognized their efforts. I've treated them like idiots and they behaved towards me in the same way that I treated them. My, I've got a lot to learn... a lot to learn.

Manager. You are absolutely right, you have got a lot to learn... and you are learning. So let's just summarize what you have learned from this recent experience. I would really appreciate it if you could do that now...

Rachel. I could and I'd like to try. First of all what strikes me is that I've judged these people on the basis that I knew the best way to run the chocolate line and they did not. I also now realize that putting them down and blaming them actually blocked my desire to achieve the twin objectives of achieving personal responsibility and self-motivation on the shifts. Most of all I have learned that people are not stupid.

Manager. Thanks for being so honest with yourself, Rachel. You have learned many things from your experience as a trainee, that's good. These learnings have presented you with a great gift and I wonder if you know what that is?

Rachel. Umm, I'm not quite sure about what you mean.

Manager. I mean that your learnings are like a gift to you, as a trainee manager. I wonder if you now can see what it means to you...

Rachel. Yes... OK. I've got you now. The biggest gift to me is the sudden realization that the people I'm learning to manage at work have the same needs as me... and...

Manager. And those needs are...?

Rachel. The need for recognition, status – that sort of thing. The need to belong and be part of what is important. Yes, I'd say the need to be considered and seen as being important and even the need to receive affection and feel included in the way I manage them.

Manager. Rachel, I would like to tell you something... You have found a great gift, for you have found out something about managing people at work that many managers never find out in a lifetime of managing others. You seem to have discovered how important it is to empower others when you are managing them and not just to try and use your position and power to get people to perform at work... Is that right?

Rachel. Yes, that is right, absolutely right, and I will tell you something else I would like to discover how I can better manage people by liberating and utilizing their abilities and concerns. I'm so excited – to me it's... it's... like a real gift, a whole new way of managing people is opening up to me. I'd never thought about managing people as empowering them, giving them power. But now I've got a thirst for it and I'd like to learn more about it and how it is done.

Manager. Rachel, I feel if we started by looking more carefully at your personal style and how you could enhance your ability to better empower the people you are managing... that would be a good place to begin, would it not?

Rachel. The sooner the better as far as I am concerned.

Example 4

Sonia, a single 37-year-old supervisor in an electronics firm who has a higher than average frequency and percentage of soldering errors in her department.

Manager. Please sit down, Sonia. You know I called you in because of the higher than average faults in the units that seem to be passing through your soldering section. What I would like us to do right now is to get a better understanding of how this is coming about and what we might do about it. Sonia, you and I have both heard the rumour that you are not up to the job... But I'd like to hear what you think and feel about these errors. Where would you like to begin?

Sonia. You know it's not my fault, there are just too many units in too short a time and the people on my team can't cope with it anymore. As for me, I don't have time to do as many inspections as I used to.

Manager. Yes, there was a point when you had more time for inspecting and when less faulty units were coming through the production line... I wonder if you know what was so different then... Sonia?

Sonia. Those were the good old days – well not all good but in those days I had confidence in my team. Now...

Manager. Now... you don't?

Sonia. I can't say that... it would be disloyal to them.

Manager. You know, I realize your team value your loyalty and I value your loyalty as well. What would you say if you were to say you had little confidence in your team?

Sonia. If I had to say I would say that we need to trust each other more and for each person in the team to do their own inspections. Then I would only have to do spot checks every so often.

Manager. Sonia, I appreciate you being straight with me... It reminds me of the time I lost confidence in my office staff and it affected me badly at the time. But I was able to talk freely with them about it. There were some difficult decisions that needed to be made and we made them together. It made a big difference to the way we worked after that – it was worth it. Maybe you have some hard decisions of your own to make for I hear you say that you could improve the inspection rates and reduce the amount of soldering errors in these units – am I right?

Sonia. Yes – you are. I realize that we need to make some changes... I'm glad I'm not the only one who has had to struggle with keeping the trust and confidence of colleagues at work.

Manager. You're not the only one... Now what kind of changes might it be useful for you to make and how could I best support you in making them?

Sonia. I think I'd like to make a start on working with the team on sharing the inspection responsibilities and building the trust up again. I'm ready to do it – now I know I have your support.

Example 5

Trevor is 37, single and is a store sales designer for a large chain of supermarkets. He is the 'ideas' man for the company and has been pivotal in its success, but over the past six months he has not produced one new idea for the future sales strategy of the company. He has a good, trusting and nurturing relationship with his manager. Trevor has requested an urgent meeting with her.

Trevor. I had to come and talk this out with you – I feel it will go no further. The truth is I'm worried sick – no sleep at night – just worrying that I can't get any ideas for next year's sales promotions. The more I try the less seems to come. I'm all washed up like a sponge that has been squeezed until there is nothing left – I am dried up of ideas.

Manager. It sounds as if you really are tired and stuck for ideas for the next sales campaign, Trevor. I remember your last campaign – it was so brilliant. How did you feel at the time that came about... it was so original?

Trevor. Oh, you mean the Disneyland idea where each store adopted a theme from famous Disney stories and the staff dressed up as the main characters... Sure, I felt great about that... It seemed to come to me when I was daydreaming in the office one day and the days after when I began to put it down on paper and the concept followed from there on in. But I did worry about getting it right... but then I always worry about the sales campaign projects for the stores, they are so critical for our success... I get a great buzz out of people telling me how great my store sales designs are but this time it's not the same...

Manager. You know, Trevor, you are absolutely right: this time it is not the same.

Trevor. You are the first person to agree with me. Everybody else seems to think I'll produce something stunning and original... But I have tried... I'm exhausted trying to find something knew... I'm weary and exhausted and my confidence is rock-bottom.

Manager. Trevor, please do something for me. Go back to last year... what were you doing about this time and get in touch with it. Just imagine you are seeing a video recording of yourself then.... OK, now what are you doing, how are you feeling?

Trevor. Ahmm... I'm having one of my daydreams and I seem to have a smile on my face... No, not a smile – more the look you have when you are having a nice light sleep... You know, kind of resting and still getting the ideas...

Manager. You are daydreaming, resting and getting ideas.

Trevor. Mmm... (indicating yes and nodding his head).

Manager. What happens next?

Trevor. Why... I... I start gushing with these images and thoughts and working with my ideas and building the designs, playing with them on my computer... Then I start worrying at the end of all this about the size of the project and if I can get the shape right and finished on time... that's about it... the design now is just a matter of procedure but I am up against the clock...

Manager. And when you are up against the clock how does that affect you?

Trevor. I worry and I am so anxious I block out my thoughts...

Manager. So when you daydream your ideas flow and you have lots of energy but when you believe you are up against a tight deadline you become anxious and your creativity becomes blocked.

Trevor. Yes, my – yes, I can see what happens now... at least I can understand how it has all come about... but how do I get rid of the blocking?

Manager. Now we know how it comes about, Trevor, we could start to find out how you can unblock or reduce the risk of blocking your ideas in the future... What would you say to that?

Trevor. I'll try anything.... I mean it, anything... if it means I can get in touch with my ideas again.

Manager. I have a hunch you have been trying too hard to force your ideas.... You can worry after the flush of ideas comes and you can have plenty of time to worry about them then. Right now... from what you say... before our next meeting. How would you feel about just spending some time daydreaming and giving up trying to produce fresh ideas?

Trevor. You mean just fantasizing in my head and drifting along until something happens and I don't have to try?

Manager. That's right, you don't have to try.

Trevor. I can't explain it but I needed you to say that; it takes a whole load of worry off my shoulders. Somehow I feel... the pressure has gone. I have noticed I get more ideas for the business when I am not under pressure.

Analyses of personal empowerment

Look at the examples we have just covered again. Which ones do you think showed the green-fingered manager at work? How did these managers empower the people they were working with, and where did they disempower them? Look at the examples closely and decide for yourself when people felt a sense of belonging and were being empowered, nurtured, listened to and when their motivation and confidence were stimulated to better manage their personal and performance problems.

You probably recognized that they were all examples of green-fingered managers at work – except for the first example. Here Derek was managed very badly – perhaps for some companies this would even be a typical way of managing the problem of 'telling' someone they were being made redundant. So what did the manager do or not do in this case?

First of all he showed no empathy or interest in Derek as a person. Certainly, the manager was efficient and clearly task-oriented. However, the second point to note is that there was no suggestion of being person-oriented – towards Derek or his concerns. Third, there wasn't any attempt to listen to Derek. Fourth, the manager showed no interest in how Derek felt about hearing the bad news. Fifth, the manager was defensive and seemed interested only in getting what had to be done over, and quickly. Finally, the manager ran the serious risk of creating the perception that the company Derek was about to leave was an uncaring employer. Above all else, Derek would definitely take some bad feelings away from his meeting with this manager. What do you think these would be? Note them now.

Now make a personal contract with yourself about how you will practically avoid the mistakes of managing people at work the way Derek was managed. Then map out for yourself how Derek should have been managed, and how you would have managed Derek. You can get a good idea of how this could be done by using your own range of personal empowerment styles. If you are stuck that is fine: it means you are finding out how to manage people at work differently. You are challenging your own habits of a lifetime and these take time to change. It takes courage to change. Once you have the courage to be a green-fingered manager you won't want to be anything like your old self, and I can tell you this – you won't be.

Practise, practise, practise

You know the way to make sure you become a green-fingered manager? Practise, practise and practise again and when you find you are able to eradicate your old habits and replace them with your new range of personal empowerment styles – you practise some more.

Using your new-found approaches to empowering people at work is like going on a journey through Aladdin's cave. You know there are some enchanting gems of personal empowerment to be found and developed. Aladdin had a genie in the lamp that produced wondrous results and achieved fantastic goals. But first Aladdin had to work at it, and find out how to release the powerful genie. The road to becoming a green-fingered manager and empowering people at work is like that. You can achieve undreamt-of results through this fresh and innovative approach to performance counselling. When you prize and value people, their attitudes, skills and personal potential, you can empower them to achieve agreed goals and overcome their performance problems at work. But to make it work, and work well, you have to be like Aladdin. You need to work at polishing the lamp. The more you polish it the more your 'genie' will appear, and the more it does, the more competent you can become at empowering people at work. Set aside at least one period each day – two if you can – and use the time to deliberately and consciously put into practice your abilities as a green-fingered manager. At first, you may feel awkward and even embarrassed. But let that all pass – as it will – and then you will find green-fingered managing to empower people at work gets that little bit easier each day and that bit more exciting as you see the difference it makes to people and their performance.

The prize is worth the price

If you find that you falter at any point along the way, remember this: the prize is worth the price.

Some of the managers I work with on their own personal empowerment abilities have been pleasantly surprised and realized genuine practical benefits when they continuously repeat the prize is worth the price to themselves – some even hum it like a melody and it allows them to get into the rhythm of empowering people at work. It seems to act as a kind of mantra for them, a reassurance and a comfort – a signal that encourages them to be confident in using their new-found abilities. So if you need to, run the mantra through your head time after time until you find yourself at ease and being a green-fingered manager at work: the prize is worth the price, the prize is worth the price, the prize is worth the price.

Green-fingered groups

Another way to make sure that you stay green-fingered is to form green-fingered groups of managers at work. By building up cells of green-fingered managers you can exchange and nurture your new styles of empowering people at work.

Donald Hebb, a distinguished American psychologist, showed how organized behaviour followed from cells or groups of people who meet and cultivate their new skills, styles and competences. He called them 'cell assemblies'. What we are talking about here is forming 'green-fingered assemblies' of managers in groups of no more than twelve per group. With these groups you can explore, understand and act on new ways of empowering people at work. You now have a solid base on which to begin that work.

The green-fingered organization

As green-fingered assemblies of managers grow and consolidate a fascinating change can begin to take place at work. You have guessed it: your organization becomes green-fingered. You are not alone: with your colleagues you can create a critical mass of green-fingered managers that reaches out and touches the whole of your organization.

When you have enough cell assemblies of green-fingered managers at work the critical mass in your business or company can reach a point where your entire business becomes green-fingered. You can become a green-fingered organization – an organization that actively prizes people, an enterprise that cultivates and thrives on encouraging personal empowerment and engendering prize-winning performances in partnership with people at work. How individual managers get there will depend on their own timetable, their own commitment, and their willingness to make changes in the way they manage people at work. But by setting a timetable in making a personal commitment to becoming a green-fingered manager and putting your personal empowerment styles into practice, you will be well on your way.

If you feel it might take you longer to become a green-fingered manager and extend the possibilities of personal empowerment to people at work, don't give up. The ancient Taoist teachings have a saying that gives us all comfort at times when we doubt ourselves: remember, the longest journey begins with the first step! Make the journey and you will meet many other managers travelling along the way. Some will be going in your direction and others will try to persuade you to give up. And there will be others setting up and nurturing groups and growing cells and assemblies of other managers who spawn yet other cells of green-fingered managers. You can watch them and join in. For they will excite, motivate and astound you at the way they manage to empower people at work. Keep your eyes firmly fixed on this last group – you are one of them. They are the new breed – the green-fingered managers, and they know where they are going.

Steps to empowerment

1. Identify a situation in the past where you were able to empower a person or people at work to achieve an important outcome. Write it down or record it on audio or video tape.

2. Now notice specifically what you said, how you said it and the way you listened to the person/people you were empowering.

3. Next visualize yourself as you were in that situation. Pay particular attention to the movements you made in relation to them and them to you.

4. After you do this, follow the thoughts you had at the time that made the difference and how this helped you to empower them.

5. At this point gather together the way you listened, spoke, felt, thought and acted and blend them – and stay silent for a few moments or as long as it takes to integrate your learnings about empowering others (some managers do this automatically – others find it takes a little longer).

6. When you have achieved this congratulate yourself on being able to release your range of personal empowerment styles that will be useful for you in performance counselling at work and other situations where you can use them.

7. Now give yourself a special signal that only you will recognize that will release your ability to empower other people at work. You might choose an image, a sound or a personal physical signal such as pressing your two thumbs together. Managers I have worked with on developing their personal empowerment strategies have come up with some unique signals for themselves – but a common one seems to be placing one hand on top of the other and giving the hand underneath a firm and confident squeeze. Remember *your* personal empowerment releasing signal and use it. It will work for you.

8. Now run through this personal empowerment strategy for yourself several times – run it through your mind like a video

you are starring in and see yourself, hear yourself, and feel how it feels as you do it. Action replay until you become more and more able to release your personal empowerment styles using your personal empowerment releasing signal.

9. When you have done this and action-replayed it often enough to yourself specify those future situations where you will use your new personal empowerment abilities. To do this well, decide and clearly rehearse *which* specific situations you will use your personal empowerment styles on, and *how, where* and *when,* and with *whom* you will use them and to *what* effect.

10. Finally, *test* out and *review* your new personal empowerment styles in these situations and in those wider ranges of opportunities for performance counselling at work. Where you need to enhance or strengthen and maintain any specific personal empowerment abilities, go through the procedure from 1-10 again and again until you find you are becoming more and more of a green-fingered manager at work.

Assignment

1. Identify a group of interested and like-minded managers and start creating, nurturing and developing green-fingered groups in your organization.

2. Make a point of meeting frequently and regularly.

3. Use your time to share and compare your successes at empowering people at work. Share the secrets of being a green-fingered manager with other managers.

4. Demonstrate to other managers outside of your group what it means to be a green-fingered manager. Arouse their curiosity and show them how you can empower people at work.

5. Discuss with your group what it means to be a green-fingered organization.

6. Now start using your green-fingered manager groups to plan and increasingly deliver practical strategies of empowering people at work in your organization.

Further Reading and References

Argyris C, *Strategy, Change and Defensive Routines,* Pitman, London, 1985.

Bailey R, *Practical Counselling Skills,* Winslow, Bicester, Oxon, 1993.

Bailey R, *50 Activities for Developing Counselling Skills for Managers,* Gower, Aldershot, 1992.

Bailey R, *Personal Empowerment Strategies,* Peak Publications, 1993.

Bailey R, *CrisisCare,* Peak Publications, 1993.

Bandier R, *Using Your Brain for a Change,* Real People Press, 1985.

Bennis, W and Burt N, *Leaders,* Harper & Row, Cambridge, 1985.

Blackstone J and Josipovic Z, *Zen for Beginners,* Unwin, London, 1986.

Drucker P, *The Frontiers of Management,* Heinemann, London, 1986.

Easwaren E, *Meditation ,* Routledge & Kegan Paul, London, 1982.

Egan G, *The Skilled Helper,* Brookes/Cole, California, 1986.

Gawain S, *Creative Visualization,* New World, California, 1990.

Handler R and Grinder J, *Frogs into Princes,* Eden Grove, Utah, 1979.

Handy C, *Gods of Management,* Pan, London, 1985.

Handy C, *Understanding Organizations,* Penguin, London, 1986.

Handy C, *The Age of Unreason,* Business Books, London, 1989.

Margerison C, *Managerial Consulting Skills,* Gower, Aldershot, 1988.

O'Connor J & Seymour J, *Introducing Neuro-Linguistic Programming,* Crucible Publications, 1990.

Pedler M, *Action Learning In Practice,* Gower, Aldershot, 1983.

Radha, *The Zen Way to be an Effective Manager,* Management Books 2000, Didcot, 1991.

Revans R, *The Origins and Growth of Action Learning,* Chartwell-Bratt Ltd, 1982.

Rogers C, *A Way of Being,* Houghton Mifflin, Boston, 1980.

Schutz C, *Profound Simplicity,* Turnstone Books, London, 1979.

Further Information

To obtain further information on how to empower people at work and personal empowerment training contact:

The Centre of Advanced Learning
Freepost (SW8716)
London
SW1V 4BR
Tel. 0171-932 0510

Index

Index

Team Management
Practical New Approaches
Charles Margerison and Dick McCann

(PB, £9.99, 176pp, 229 x 145mm, 1-85252-114-7)

Team Management presents a new set of techniques developed by two influential thinkers and consultants, Dr Charles Margerison and Dr Dick McCann. These techniques will improve team performance and increase your business success.

Margerison and McCann have drawn on the original findings of psychologist Carl Jung and adapted his concepts to the workplace. The heart of their techniques is the Team Management Wheel - a management tool to aid self-understanding, teamwork, career development, communication and leadership.

'This book provides a new insight into understanding how people work together and is an essential handbook for managers who wish to improve cooperation and commitment within teams.'
Journal of Management Psychology

'The springboard for a radical reappraisal of the way work teams do business in your organisation.'
Quality Newsletter

Dr Margerison and Dr McCann are co-founders of the international consultancy, Team Management Systems, which promotes and supports the techniques and principles outlined in this book. Before founding TMS, Dr Margerison spent a number of years working in industry, government and education. He has been a Professor of Management at Cranfield in the UK and the University of Queensland in Australia. Dr McCann's previous experience was as a chemical engineer and in project management for the alternative energy business.

Enhancing Employee Performance

Bernard Katz & John Docherty

(PB, £9.99, 208pp, 229 x 145mm, ISBN: 1-85252-230-5

Enhancing Employee Performance is a down-to-earth, practical guide to the management techniques that encourage employees to work well and effectively, both with each other and for the customer.

Management is easiest when the setting is right, and Part 1 of the book therefore deals with ways of finding the right employee. Selection and recruitment are put in the context of the overall human resource requirements of the organization or company.

Part 2 is concerned with ways of turning staff into added-value employees. It develops a range of techniques for training, developing employee relationships, monitoring performance and what to do when things go wrong. Special attention is paid to dealing with trade unions and how to design a supportive workforce environment and organization culture.

The presentation throughout the book is in a question-and-answer format, which makes it particularly easy to identify subjects of special interest, and to help the reader to put theory into practice right away the text is supported with numerous examples, rules and checklists.

Bernard Katz, after graduating in psychology, worked in business, subsequently running and then selling his own company. He is now principal of the consultancy International Marketing Associates, providing management training services and speaker assignments in the UK, Australia, South East Asia, South Africa and South America. He is the author of seven other books on management topics.

John Docherty is a fellow of the Institute of Personnel Management and has spent 25 years in the personnel field, holding positions in the engineering, paper and board, and food industries. He is now the Foodservices Divisional Personnel and Training Manager for Rank Hovis McDougal Plc.

Available from leading booksellers.
To order by phone on 7-day trial, ring 01235-815544 now (credit cards accepted - full refund if returned in 7 days). Full catalogue available.

Peak Performance
Become More Effective at Work
Windy Dryden & Jack Gordon

(PB, £9.99, 160pp, 234mm x 156mm, ISBN: 1-85252-182-1)

An innovative self-training book introducing a new system of personal development based on the pioneering principles of "Rational-Emotive Training".

This book introduces business executives and decision-makers in industry and government to a new research-tested way of thinking, feeling and acting, designed to maximise their executive ability to cope efficiently with the every day problems and hassles of the organisational world, and to operate both their business and personal life with minimum stress and maximum satisfaction.

Peak Performance will help readers to cut their way through the emotional problems and other personal pressures and blocks which get in the way of achieving optimum results for themselves and their organisations.

ABOUT THE AUTHOR

Windy Dryden is a senior lecturer in psychology at Goldsmiths' College, University of London. He has written or edited 40 books and over 120 articles and book chapters. He is Britain's leading counselling psychologist and counsellor educator.

Jack Gordon has worked in a variety of management jobs in government and private companies. He has trained in Rational-Emotive psychotherapy (RET) and has co-authored with Windy Dryden a practitioner's manual entitled "What is Rational-Emotive Therapy?"

'Presents the principles and practices of rational emotive therapy (REP)' *Business Executive*

Who Cares Wins

How to unlock the hidden potential in people at work

Peter Savage

(PB, £6.99, 144pp, 234 x 156mm, ISBN: 1-85252-015-9)

Today's winning company is without question the one that utilises the men and women a its disposal more effectively than its competitors can utilise theirs. Peter Savage's step-by-step outline of the key to effective man management looks at the problems and challenges confronting managers and supervisors at every level and considers how recent theories of 'excellence' can be transformed into practical profitable reality. He explains how to create a platform for change and how to use it to unlock crucial hidden energy from colleagues and employees with spectacular results.

Peter Savage joined industry in 1965 with an honours degree in Chemistry. He has worked as a director responsible for a European plastics business within an American chemical company. In 1988, he became a main board director of a major British plc, in charge of their chemicals division.

His work has involved him in the leadership and management of major change programmes in large manufacturing and international commercial environments – a subject on which he frequently lectures.

'Carefully and convincingly argued, with sound exemplary support details, clearly written and well referenced' Dr Allan Jackson, *MBA Review.*